ROAD TO BAGHDAD
IRAQ 2003

A FORCE ON FORCE COMPANION

AMBUSH ALLEY GAMES

OSPREY
PUBLISHING

First published in Great Britain in 2011 by Osprey Publishing Ltd.

Osprey Publishing
Midland House, West Way, Botley, Oxford, OX2 0PH, UK
44–02 23rd St, Suite 219, Long Island City, NY 11101, USA
E-mail: info@ospreypublishing.com

Ambush Alley Games LLC
1792 Denim Lane, Enid, OK 73703, USA
E-mail: info@ambushalleygames.com

A CIP catalog record for this book is available from the British Library

Print ISBN: 978 1 84908 517 5
PDF e-book ISBN: 978 1 84908 519 9

Lead Authors: Leigh Neville
Supporting Authors: Robby Carpenter, Jim Roots, Jim Wonacott, Shawn Carpenter
Original USMC Scenarios created by: D. Chris Sebolt, Jerry Lannigan
AAG Editors: Shawn Carpenter and Peggy Carpenter, with thanks to Kathy Murphy

Play-Testers: Andy Rix, Chris Mihlan, Christopher Maes, Jason Mastros, Lex Shorey, Alex Shorey, Rene Raap, Rutger van Marissing, Shaun Matthews, Stephen Crawford, Steve Morris, Tom Konczal & The Mid-America Wargamers, Cyril Vallin, Jake Rose, Jim Roots, Jose Ventura, Michael Moore, Piers Brand, Rich Chambers

Miniatures photos by Piers Brand unless otherwise noted. Models and scenery from the collections of Piers Brand and Justin Powles.
Photos by US Dept. of Defense, Michael Moore, and Erik Emmerson
Maps by Shawn Carpenter

Cover concept and page layout by Myriam Bell Design, France
Cover artwork by Ramiro Bujeiro
Typeset in Bank Gothic and Minion Pro
Originated by PDQ Media, Bungay, UK
Printed in China through Worldprint

11 12 13 14 15   10 9 8 7 6 5 4 3 2 1

Osprey Publishing is supporting the Woodland Trust, the UK's leading woodland conservation charity, by funding the dedication of trees.

www.ospreypublishing.com

For more information on *Force On Force* and other products, please visit www.ambushalleygames.com

TABLE OF CONTENTS

INTRODUCTION

Road to Baghdad, the first companion book for *Force on Force*, is somewhat of a "coming home" project. Our original rule set, *Ambush Alley* was written specifically to evoke the frantic clashes between well trained, technologically superior troops and highly motivated, poorly trained and equipped insurgents that characterized most of the engagements during the "march up-country" to Baghdad. As a result, you'll find more "asymmetric" scenarios in this book than you'll see in many others.

It is our intent in this book to provide wargamers with a glimpse into the Coalition operations that struck Saddam Hussein's regime like a thunderbolt and whet your appetites for further research into this brief but fascinating chapter in military history. Within these pages you'll find a selection of scenarios representative of the actions that characterized Operation *Cobra II* up until the fall of Baghdad, along with organization guidelines for the forces involved in the conflict and write-ups for the vehicles they operated – basically everything you need to bring this theater to your tabletop!

This book owes its existence to the talent and diligence of several authors, whom we'd like to recognize for their specific contributions.

- Chris Sebolt and Jerry Lanigan compiled the original drafts of eight of the scenarios presented in *Marching Up-Country with the USMC*. We're extremely grateful to Chris and Jerry for providing the solid foundation upon which we built our versions of these excellent scenarios.
- Leigh Neville and Jim Wonacott revised the Sebolt/Lanigan scenarios and contributed their own scenarios as well. Leigh and Jim have left their stamp of military knowledge and scenario design excellence all over this project.
- Jim Roots (The Other Jim) contributed a concise and incisive historical treatment of the events leading to the fall of Baghdad which can be found in *The Road to Baghdad: An Unprecedented Journey*.
- Thanks also to Matt from Elheim Miniatures, Shaun from S&S Models, Eric Hotz of Hotz ArtWorks, and Brian from TheHobbyDen for their assistance in making the miniatures photos in this book possible!

We hope you enjoy *Road to Baghdad* as much as we've enjoyed bringing it to you!

Ambush Alley Games

THE ROAD TO BAGHDAD: AN UNPRECEDENTED JOURNEY

The road to Baghdad traversed twenty-one days of unprecedented military accomplishments. Arguably, the road represents the most rapid advance in the history of warfare. Littered along that road are many tales of courage, some of which are recreated in this book; but just as many tales of indecision, unexpected occurrences and tragedy. It was a war of maneuver punctuated with sharp, fierce fights that ended as quickly as they began. It was a war of brutal city fighting and sieges unplanned for by the US-led coalition. It was a war of imbalance, with the defenders greatly outnumbering the attackers, who also had to contend with an accelerated timetable for their ground action.

For many Americans, the Iraq War was a war in their living rooms. It was a war of words and speculation. It was not the casualty lists or canned footage of Vietnam, but live images courtesy of embedded news crews featuring tanks and APCs rolling across the desert, interrupted by the constant commentary of pundits ranging from retired generals to largely uninformed media celebrities.

Finally, the war along the road to Baghdad ended Saddam Hussein's regime, but was largely ignored by most Iraqis. The best summary may be John Keegan's decision to call the war "mysterious in almost every aspect."[1]

1 John Keegan, *The Iraq War*, p.2. Vintage Books, ©2005

A PRELUDE TO WAR

There were many pretexts for the United States to invade Iraq with the goal of taking Baghdad and bringing down the government of Saddam Hussein. Unfinished business from the Gulf War, alleged weapons of mass destruction (WMDs), oppression of the Iraqi people, defiance of UN and US ultimatums...the list goes on. Many of these *casus belli* are still hotly debated. The fact of the matter is that a predominantly US force, assisted by the British and other NATO nations, invaded Iraq on March 19, 2003.

The US Congress authorized President Bush to use military force against Iraq in October 2002. The military buildup had already begun prior to that date, however. US and British aircraft began systematically bombing air defense sites in the no-fly zones established after the Gulf War earlier in the year. CIA Special Activities Division (SAD) teams were operating in the northern part of

HH-60L MEDEVAC
HELICOPTER, IRAQ, 2003

Iraq as early as July 2002 with assistance from the Army's 10th Special Forces Group (10th SFG).

General Tommy Franks was chosen to command the invasion. A Vietnam veteran, a key strategist of the Gulf War and fresh from success in Afghanistan where he used special operations forces to topple the Taliban, he seemed the perfect choice. His objectives were the capture of the Iraqi oil infrastructure intact; discovery and neutralization of WMDs; and the capture of Baghdad.

Franks was not in favor of a massive buildup as seen in the previous Gulf War. He intended to achieve operational surprise against the Iraqi military by striking more quickly than General Schwarzkopf. His experience in commanding integrated air and special forces assets in Afghanistan led him to believe that economy of force and integration between the different combat arms, supplemented by special forces, could best achieve his objectives.

US CENTCOM felt that the current geopolitical situation eliminated Saudi Arabia as a staging area, a luxury they'd enjoyed in the first Gulf War. This meant that Iraqi

forces could be concentrated against a few likely invasion routes. Franks' initial plan called for a two-pronged attack featuring the 4th Infantry Division staging in Turkey and attacking Baghdad from the north with the *coup de main* starting from Kuwait and attacking from the south. This had the advantage of tying down significant Iraqi forces away from the main thrust. The plan had to be abandoned when Turkey announced its unwillingness to be used as a staging area for either air or ground assets, despite its membership in NATO. Franks needed another plan to tie down the Iraqis.

FRANKS' PLAN: COBRA II

"Let me begin by saying that this will be a campaign unlike any other in history, a campaign characterized by shock, by surprise, by the employment of precise munitions on a scale never seen, and by the application of overwhelming force."

- Gen. Tommy Franks, 22 March 2003, CentCom daily briefing

Franks and CENTCOM's final operational plan, codenamed *Cobra II*, kept the main southern thrust intact. Wanting to avoid the obvious assault route into Iraq, the area between the Tigris and Euphrates Rivers, Franks elected for his main force, the US Fifth Corps, spearheaded by the 3rd Infantry Division, to swing around the main occupied areas and attack Baghdad from west of the Euphrates. The 1st Marine Expeditionary Force (1st MEF) was to feint to the east, then drive alongside Fifth Corps to the east of the Euphrates, protecting the flank of the invasion. 1st MEF was to keep pace with the Army units and to avoid urban engagements in the inhabited regions between the Tigris and Euphrates. Paralleling the

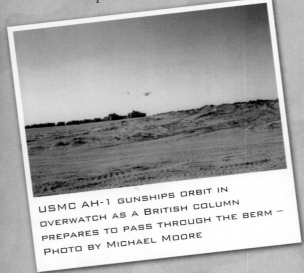

USMC AH-1 GUNSHIPS ORBIT IN OVERWATCH AS A BRITISH COLUMN PREPARES TO PASS THROUGH THE BERM — PHOTO BY MICHAEL MOORE

advance of 1st MEF was another Marine unit, Task Force Tarawa, which was given the mission of protecting the eastern flank of the Marines. A secondary thrust by the 1st MEF was planned toward the ports of Umm Qasr and Basra, featuring the US 15th Marine Expeditionary Unit, the British 1st UK Armored Division and other coalition forces. This action was designed to secure the vital oil and harbor facilities in the area.

The second part of Franks' plans involved special operations forces in the north and west of Iraq. In the north, CIA Special Activities Division (SAD) teams and SOF worked with Kurdish irregulars to tie down Iraqi forces. In the west, SOF teams went "scud hunting" to prohibit Iraqi retaliatory strikes toward Coalition-friendly nations.

The plan made the best use of available forces and hinged upon combined arms, not only of air/artillery/ground/armor assets within services, but inter-service and inter-nation coordinated planning and execution.

HIGH LEVEL ORDERS OF BATTLE

Unlike the Gulf War, the Coalition this time around was predominantly comprised of US forces. Many nations, including NATO members, did not support the invasion and refused to provide military support. Participating nations included Australia, Denmark, Poland, Portugal, Spain and the United Kingdom.

COALITION FORCES
US FIFTH CORPS
- 3rd Infantry Division (mechanized)
- 101st Airborne
- 2nd Brigade, 82nd Airborne
- 4th Infantry Division
- 173rd Airborne Brigade

1ST MARINE EXPEDITIONARY FORCE
- 1st Marine Division
- Task Force Tarawa (elements from 1st and 2nd Marine Division)
- 1st UK Armored Division
- Royal Marine Commando Brigade
- British 16th Air Assault Brigade

SPECIAL OPERATIONS FORCES
- 5th Special Forces Group (southern and western Iraq)
- 10th Special Forces Group (northern Iraq)
- 3rd Special Forces Group (northern Iraq)
- Joint Special Operations Command (Task Force 20) (western Iraq)
- British, Australian, Polish contingents (western and southern Iraq)

IRAQI FORCES
Information about the Iraqi forces is less available and less reliable. Many of their units disintegrated at first contact with Coalition forces. The following is their Order of Battle just before the war.

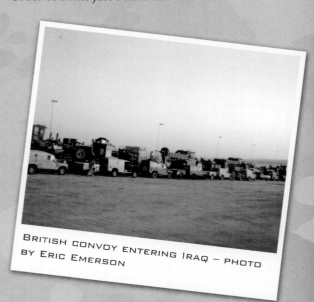

BRITISH CONVOY ENTERING IRAQ – PHOTO BY ERIC EMERSON

REPUBLICAN GUARD

Northern Corps

- 2nd Al Medina Armored Division
- 5th Baghdad Mechanized Division
- 7th Adnan Infantry Division

Southern Corps

- Al Naida Infantry Division
- 6th Nebuchadnezzer Mechanized Division
- 1st Hammurabi Infantry Division

Miscellaneous

- As Saiqa Special Forces Division (3+ brigades)
- Special Republican Guard (4 brigades)

REGULAR ARMY

1st Corps (centered near Kirkuk)

- 5th Mechanized Division
- 2nd Infantry Division
- 8th Infantry Division
- 38th Infantry Division

2nd Corps (near Diyala)

- 3rd Armored Division
- 15th Infantry Division
- 34th Infantry Division

3rd Corps (An Nasiriya)

- 6th Armored Division
- 51st Mechanized Division
- 11th Infantry Division

4th Corps (Amara)

- 10th Armored Division
- 14th Infantry Division
- 18th Infantry Division

BRITISH CHALLENGERS "BOMBING UP" BEFORE ENTERING IRAQ. – PHOTO BY MICHAEL MOORE

5th Corps (near Mosul)

- 1st Mechanized Division
- 4th Infantry Division
- 7th Infantry Division
- 16th Infantry Division

WESTERN DESERT FORCE

- Miscellaneous mixed armored and infantry units operating in Western Iraq

FEDAYEEN

- Largely Sunni and Ba'ath party irregular forces from Iraq, supplemented by Syrian and Egyptian sympathizers

AN ACCELERATED TIMETABLE

Forces were still in route to Iraq, particularly the 4th Infantry Division once Turkey denied it a base of operations, when the timetable for invasion was moved up. It had always been a part of Franks' strategy to move with fewer forces and more speed than the past Gulf War. Prior campaigns were preceded by long periods of aerial bombardment. Franks wanted a short, intensive air campaign followed by a lightning ground campaign to achieve tactical, even operational surprise. Even

Franks' definition of "short" was challenged by the marching orders that came from Washington following the March 19 "decapitation strike" that went awry.

CIA sources inside Iraq supposedly determined the location of high-level Iraqi officials, including Saddam Hussein, and President Bush seized the opportunity to launch a crippling blow against the Iraqi leadership. Two F-117s delivered four precision-guidance bombs and six ships launched more than forty cruise missiles against an underground bunker in Baghdad where Saddam and his leadership were allegedly meeting. The information proved incorrect, and the Iraqis quickly used the failed strike as an opportunity to heat up the propaganda war and to launch a retaliatory SCUD strike against Coalition forces in Kuwait (to no effect). In the aftermath of the failed attack, Franks got word to set the invasion in motion.

THE INITIAL CLASHES: MARCH 20–21

Fifth Corps, with the 3rd Infantry Division in the van, crossed the border and began its western sweep toward Baghdad. Resistance was light, with many Iraqi formations simply disintegrating or surrendering en masse to the advancing Americans. The main elements of the 1st MEF also advanced into Iraq, while amphibious

DORA FARMS

The "Decapitation Strike" against "Rocket One" (as Hussein was dubbed by the USAF) was meant to end the war before it had begun. Instead, the combined F-117 and Tomahawk strike struck an empty field at Dora Farms, a retreat which Iraqi insiders stated that Hussein had not visited in eight years.

The end result of the attack shouldn't detract from the herculean efforts required to bring the strike to bear, however. Despite communications failures and overwhelming logistics hurdles, the USAF and USN was able to coordinate a combined attack with a startlingly short lead-time. The craters at Dora Farms prove that, with accurate intelligence, devastatingly effective strikes can be orchestrated within a tactically meaningful time-frame.

operations featuring the 15th Marine Expeditionary Unit and British Royal Marine Commandos began against the Al Faw peninsula to secure oil fields and ultimately capture Umm Qasr and Basra.

Umm Qasr was the first determined resistance of the campaign. US Marines initially captured the port facilities on March 21 (see **Scenario 2: Umm Qasr**), but it would take several more days of intensive action by allied troops to secure the town from Iraqi troops.

A special job was given to the 1st Battalion, 7th Marine Regiment, 1st Marine Division; the capture of the pumping station at the Rumaila oil fields (see **Scenario 1:**

CHALLENGER 2 MBT, BASRA, 2003

US MARINES FROM THE 15TH MEUSOC DURING THE FIGHTING AT UMM QASR

The Crown Jewel). This assault was designed to preserve the critical oil infrastructure of Iraq, since more than 50% of the country's oil flowed through this facility.

The 1st UK Armored Division reached the outskirts of Basra and cordoned off the city, but allowed civilians to leave. The British met stiff resistance from Iraqi regulars and the Fedayeen under the command of Ali Hassan Al Majid, one of Saddam's chief lieutenants and better known as "Chemical Ali." The British pace of operations led to criticism from US commanders, since the Coalition plan of attack was based on speed to keep the enemy off balance. The British, however, were determined to minimize casualties for a war that was unpopular at home. Basra would become a major battleground over the next two weeks.

A RAPID ADVANCE AND A WRONG TURN: MARCH 22–25

The thrust by US Fifth Corps was far more rapid than anyone anticipated. Many Iraqi units stationed in its path simply disappeared, either through covert negotiations with the Iraqi commanders prior to hostilities, through fear or through lack of support. Many soldiers simply threw away their uniforms and equipment, exchanging them for civilian garb. The 1st MEF experienced the same mass surrenders during its initial advance. By the end of the day on March 22, lead elements of Fifth Corps were 150 miles inside Iraq, almost exactly halfway to Baghdad (see **Scenario 11: The Hornet's Nest**).

Keeping the troops supplied in the field was no small feat, and one of the greatest achievements of the war was the performance of US logistics. US columns on the march would halt at predetermined checkpoints and suddenly be swarmed by resupply vehicles and in a matter of an hour or two, be on their way again. Huge credit goes to US planning and GPS navigation. But sometimes things don't go as intended. The unfortunate fate of the 507th Maintenance Battalion is a prime example.

During the advance to Baghdad, the three columns of Fifth Corps, 1st MEF and Task Force Tarawa converged near Nasiriya. This city was a major crossing over the Euphrates and home to the Iraqi 11th Infantry Division. Pre-war planning called for the Marines of Task Force Tarawa to seize only eastern portions of the city and its bridges in order to secure convoy routes. In hindsight, the plan seems implausible, since any convoys attempting to pass through An Nasiriya would be subject to harassing fire. In fact, the route through the city was already nicknamed "Ambush Alley" by Marine planners. But the mood in US CENTCOM was optimistic; intelligence indicated that the Iraqi 11th Division had withdrawn and only light resistance was expected. Orders to Task Force Tarawa were to move on their objective quickly.

On the morning of March 23, a convoy of the 507th Maintenance Battalion, moving to resupply the US 3rd Infantry Division, took a wrong turn and headed for the eastern bridge in An Nasiriya. The column was shot up badly, with nine killed and six captured, including Jessica Lynch. Task Force Tarawa, already planning to assault the eastern bridge, quickly sent its 1st Battalion, 2nd Marines to the rescue of the 507th's ambushed column (see **Scenario 3: CAAT Fight Near Nasiriya**).

What the Marines discovered in An Nasiriya was that the city was anything but unoccupied. Buses, cars, taxis and motorcycles full of Fedayeen fighters, comprised of Iraqis, Syrians, Egyptians, Palestinians and even Chechens, desiring to test their mettle against the Americans, arrived in An Nasiriya in droves. Task Force Tarawa's lead elements found themselves in a battle they hadn't planned (see **Scenario 4: The Railroad Bridge**).

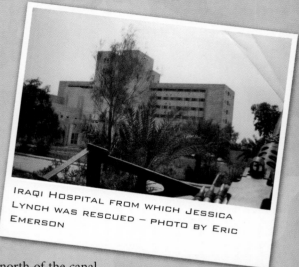

IRAQI HOSPITAL FROM WHICH JESSICA LYNCH WAS RESCUED – PHOTO BY ERIC EMERSON

AMBUSH ALLEY: MARCH 23

Compounding matters, Task Force Tarawa went into action piecemeal and with poor coordination. A Company of 1/2 Marines seized the eastern bridge. But B Company passed through them, then took a wrong side road and found itself first in a firefight, then stuck in place as several of its vehicles became bogged in mud and refuse. C, or "Charlie" Company took up the advance to the Saddam Canal bridge through Ambush Alley.

In perhaps the most famous ground action of the war, Charlie Company advanced over the bridge, but an RPG hit one of its AAVP personnel carriers ("Tuna Boats" in Marine slang). The vehicle managed to cross the bridge, but its exterior gear was on fire and its loading ramp was jammed. Marines were jumping out of the escape hatches. There were still wounded Marines inside. Charlie Company now found itself straddling the canal, with seven AAVPs on the north side of the canal and four on the other, taking fire from Fedayeen and Iraqi mortars.

Yet more tragedy was to come, largely caused by malfunctioning radios, poor inter-unit communications and bad radio discipline in the battalion net. A Marine forward air controller, believing there to be no Marines north of the canal, mistakenly directed A-10s to strafe Charlie Company's vehicles north of the canal. Several passes later, multiple AAVPs were damaged and one destroyed, with six Marines killed due to friendly fire (see **Scenario 5: Ambush Alley**).

With casualties mounting and no MEDEVAC possible due to the Iraqi/Fedayeen fire, Charlie Company decided to send six of its AAVPs back down Ambush Alley to help. On the way, it staggered into another Fedayeen ambush, losing two AAVPs destroyed and two more severely damaged. Many of the Marines were killed or wounded. South of the bridge, some of these beleaguered Charlie Company survivors holed up in a building dubbed "The Alamo" (see **Scenario 6: The Alamo**). Described by many survivors as another Mogadishu, the Marines held off numerous assaults until finally relieved by an Abrams and two Humvees after several hours of isolation.

Other actions were conducted by Task Force Tarawa to get forces moving toward Al Kut, and An Nasiriya was eventually surrounded by the task force to cut off outside reinforcements, but it would be April before the town was fully pacified.

BUMPS ON THE ROAD TO BAGHDAD: MARCH 25–27

While Task Force Tarawa was heavily engaged at An Nasiriya, the Coalition was experiencing other difficulties. The British had laid siege to Basra, but during this period in time, refused to engage the Iraqi forces in the city other than small raids by the SAS and Royal Marines. The British instead waited out the Iraqis and laid the intelligence groundwork for later action. Some elements of the media chose to point to this as a stalemate and lumped it together with An Nasiriya as evidence that the war was not going as well as planned.

Meanwhile the US 3rd Infantry Division was on the outskirts of Najaf. It was here that the 11th Helicopter Regiment, operating in support of the 3rd ID attempted to engage the Al Medina Armored Division of the Republican Guard with a massed attack by 32 Apache helicopters. A combination of bad weather, poor communications and surprisingly intense ground fire resulted in the loss of one Apache and significant damage to many others.

The weather, too, decided to add impediments to the Iraqi battlefield. On March 25 an intense sandstorm arose, followed by torrential rains. Some observers said it was the worst

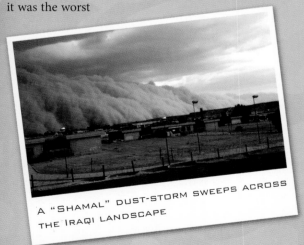

A "SHAMAL" DUST-STORM SWEEPS ACROSS THE IRAQI LANDSCAPE

storm of its kind in over 100 years, with 50-mile-an-hour winds. It slowed down the advancing troops and imposed an operational pause on the Coalition.

By this time, it was also becoming apparent that the regular Iraqi army was not willing to fight. While the majority of the Republican Guard still lay ahead of the paths of Fifth Corps and 1st MEF, and was still a major operational consideration, the real enemies were the groups of Fedayeen. In a foreshadowing of the insurgency to come, small units of fanatical irregulars were attacking both Coalition front line troops and logistics columns. In the interest of security, more urban actions were necessary along convoy routes than initially planned.

GETTING READY: MARCH 26–30

A crucial meeting took place on March 26 at 1st MEF's headquarters. The American top commanders flew in for a conference to determine the next steps on the road to Baghdad. The Coalition forces were facing several major issues. First, supply was getting critical for 3rd Infantry Division and supply routes were still uncertain given the situation at An Nasiriya. Second, too much combat power of 3rd Infantry Division, 1st MEF and Task Force Tarawa was getting tied up in secondary actions at places like An Nasiriya, Samawa and Najaf. The decision was made to employ 82nd and 101st Airborne troops to secure the route between An Nasiriya and Najaf, allowing 3rd Infantry Division to gather its strength and push forward to the Karbala Gap, its final objective before the assault on Baghdad proper.

Following the main actions at An Nasiriya, the Marines raced to get into position astride Fifth Corps for the final push to Baghdad. Eager to press on, 1st MEF and Task Force Tarawa seize objective after objective, pausing neither for the sandstorm, traditional resupply (on one occasion the Marines arrange to have C-130s land on Route 1 with 5,000 gallon containers of fuel) nor Iraqi settlements. Commencing with the town of Afak on March 29, the Marines invented "the Afak drill," whereby they approach a town with overwhelming firepower to its front and pinned defenders in place, while tanks and infantry envelop the flanks (see **Scenario 7: The Afak Drill**). The tactic worked so well it became standard procedure for the rest of the march to Baghdad.

Meanwhile in northern Iraq, the 173rd Airborne Brigade and the 10th Special Forces Group were causing havoc for the Iraqis. Working with Kurdish *Peshmerga* ('those who face death'), these units managed to tie down the Iraqi 5th Corps and keep it from moving against the Coalition advance toward Baghdad.

The inexorable advance of the 1st MEFs regimental combat teams (RCTs) convinced Iraqi commanders that the main assault against Baghdad was to come from the south, the traditional route of attack (see **Scenario 9: Al Kut**). The Marines had other plans. They feinted north, then swung due east, crossed the Euphrates and approached Baghdad from the southeast.

Fifth Corps also staged a number of deceptions which kept Iraqi leadership unsure about the direction of its main effort. Two Brigade Combat Teams (BCTs) of 3rd Infantry Division, with 7th Cavalry in the lead, attacked through to the Karbala Gap. The remainder of the division, along with the 101st, made demonstration attacks to keep the Iraqis guessing about what was going to happen next.

MEANWHILE, IN BASRA

While the Fifth Corps and 1st MEF moved against Baghdad, the British were not idle in the south. The British Royal Marine Commando Brigade remained to hold Umm Qasr and the Al Faw peninsula, giving the job of isolating and clearing the city of Basra to the 1st UK Armored Division. Seizing control of all routes into the city, the British methodically shut down the

ABRAMS TANKS ADVANCE ACROSS THE DESERT. — PHOTO BY MICHAEL MOORE

Iraqis ability to resist, although not without meeting stiff resistance from the Iraqi regulars and irregulars under siege. One notable action took place on March 27, when 14 Challenger II tanks of the Royal Scots Guard Dragoons, part of the 7th Armored Brigade (the famed Desert Rats) met and destroyed 14 Iraqi tanks in the largest British tank battle since World War II.

On April 6 the British stormed the remainder of the city, ending the battle for Basra.

OPERATIONS IN THE WESTERN DESERT

Just as in the Gulf War, Special Forces teams from the US, Britain and Australia operated in Iraq's western desert to interdict the flow of foreign aid and manpower to Iraq as well as locate launch sites and potential sites of WMDs. These included elements of the 5th Special Forces Group, JSOC's Task Force 20, Australian SASR and UK 22SAS and SBS. Iraq still had a large number of SCUD launchers capable of hitting Coalition forces and friendly nations. Thanks to the successes of these teams, the SCUD threat was practically non-existent.

SADDAM – MAKE THAT *BAGHDAD* – INTERNATIONAL AIRPORT

With the attention of the Iraqi leadership focused on 1st MEF and 5th Corps diversions, the main body of 3rd Infantry Division fought through the Karbala Gap on April 1 and April 2. Helped by Special Forces and close air support, the leading elements crossed the Euphrates north of Karbala and assaulted the remnants of the Republican Guard Medina Division. A major hole was now open in the Iraqi lines. Desperate to repulse the Americans, the Iraqi leadership hurled repeated assaults at the bridgehead by Fedayeen to no avail. On April 4, 3rd Infantry's 1st Brigade engaged defenders at the Saddam International Airport during several hours of fierce fighting (**see Scenario 13: Medal of Honor**) in perhaps the heaviest action of the war. Following the end of the war, the airport was renamed Baghdad International Airport.

THE RAT IS BACK! – PHOTO BY MICHAEL MOORE

CHALLENGER ARMOURED REPAIR AND RECOVERY VEHICLE, AL FAW PENINSULA, 2003

THUNDER RUNS: APRIL 5 AND 7

Many Iraqi commanders later admitted that the fall of the airport was the last truly organized resistance prior to the fall of Baghdad. However, that did not mean there were not significant forces and skirmishes to come. With the airport in Coalition hands, 3rd Infantry Division decided to test the remaining Baghdad defenses with a reconnaissance in force by a task force of its 2nd Brigade. The term "Thunder Run" was coined to describe the activity. Advancing from the south on April 5, the task force met with little organized resistance, although there were a few intense firefights along the way. Based on the success of the first Thunder Run, a second one set out on April 7 comprised of the entirety of 2nd Brigade. It succeeded in reaching the government district of the capital and capturing what is today called the Green Zone.

That same day Marines crossed the Diyala River into the southern part of the capital (see **Scenario 10: The Footbridge**) and elements of 3rd Infantry Division captured one of Saddam's palaces and the Coalition called upon the Iraqis to surrender.

THE FALL OF BAGHDAD AND THE END OF THE ROAD

Coalition forces formally occupied Baghdad on April 9, concluding an amazing 21 days of combat operations. The road to Baghdad ended in a Coalition military victory. But the path to peace was just beginning. Almost from the start of the occupation, signs that things weren't going to be easy began to appear. Looting was rampant throughout Baghdad, not just of Saddam's palaces and possessions, but of Iraqi cultural treasures. The infrastructure of the city, not well maintained by Saddam during his reign, crumbled under the additional stresses of war and occupation. More significantly, many political leaders, including Saddam himself, fled the city to either go into hiding or become members of the nascent insurgency.

The Coalition's quick victory would be rewarded with seven years of counter-insurgency efforts and nation building before a new Iraq was deemed ready to take responsibility for its own governance and security. Only time will tell how much longer Coalition involvement will be required to see Iraq transition from despotic dictatorship to a fully functioning democracy.

A CSAR FLIGHT OVER OCCUPIED BAGHDAD

MARCHING UP-COUNTRY WITH THE USMC

SCENARIO 1: THE CROWN JEWEL

Az Zubayr, March 21

The 1st Battalion 7th Marines was handed a critical mission early in Operation Iraqi Freedom. The pumping station at Az Zubayr receives oil from throughout the Rumaila oil fields for storage or transport to the al Faw Peninsula. The destruction of this station, responsible for over $40 million in oil per day, would cripple recovery efforts and potentially lead to an environmental disaster of massive proportions. Rather than hand the operation to SOF, the Marine battalion was tasked with securing it and surrounding storage units. Two squads of carefully trained Marines were to secure the station itself by *coup de main*. Unfortunately, the number and quality of defenders were unknown.

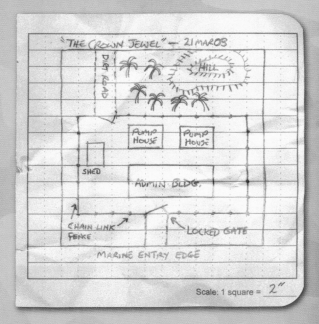

Scale: 1 square = 2"

HISTORICAL OUTCOME

The reality of the battle for the Crown Jewel was much less dramatic than the scenario presented here. The Marines encountered no resistance at Az Zubayr, finding the facility guarded by a lone elderly watchman and a number of civilian workers who surrendered immediately. The only other "inhabitant" of the Crown Jewel was an unfortunate technician who had been beheaded by Ba'ath officials before they fled the site to discourage cooperation with Coalition forces. The Marines then called in both British Army reservists who were oil technology experts in their civilian life and the CIA recruited Iraqis to assess the limited damage the Ba'ath Party members had inflicted. The Crown Jewel had been captured intact with no Coalition losses.

SCENARIO INFORMATION

Duration of Game: 6 Turns

Initiative: USMC has Initiative for duration of game

Special Conditions:

- Fedayeen are Irregulars
- Air Defense Environment: Light Air Defense

Fog of War: Determined normally by Reaction Test rolls

Special Assets:

USMC: 1 x AH-1W Whisky Cobra available on-station in direct support from Turn 2. Use standard FOF air rules with a TQ roll each turn to keep it on the table, otherwise called away to another tasking or gone Winchester/Bingo in ordnance/fuel state.

Table Size: 2' x 2'
- Note that the pump houses are 6" behind the main building.

USMC MISSION

Marine Corporal Ferkovich is Force Commander for this mission. Your squad is charged with breaching the security fence surrounding the facility and neutralizing all threats to your Marines and to the facility's function. Maps of the area have been provided by intelligence, but little concrete information is available regarding enemy strength and disposition. Intel reports do cite recent movement of Fedayeen Saddam and Ba'athist elements near the facility. Their activities, numbers and weapons are unknown at this time. The Crown Jewel must be seized intact to allow Coalition experts to assess any damage caused to the pumping station.

USMC VICTORY POINTS
- Seize the pumping turbines at Az Zubayr before they can be destroyed by Iraqi forces: 5pts
- No KIA or POW Marines at end of Turn 6: 3pts

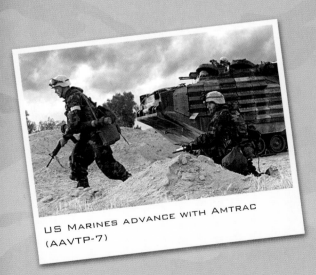

US MARINES ADVANCE WITH AMTRAC (AAVTP-7)

USMC FORCE

USMC Basic Attributes
Initiative Level: N/A
Confidence Level: High
Supply Level: Normal
Body Armor: Standard (1D)
Troop Quality/Morale: D8/D10

USMC Rifle Squad One (Equipped with Breaching Kit)
1 x Squad Leader w/M16A2 (Cpl. Ferkovich)

Fire Team One Alpha
1 x Fire Team Leader w/M16A2
1 x Grenadier w/M203 (Lt. AP:1/AT:0)
1 x Gunner w/M249 (Lt. AP:1/AT:0)
1 x Rifleman w/M16A2

Fire Team One Bravo
1 x Fire Team Leader w/M16A2
1 x Grenadier w/M203 (Lt. AP:1/AT:0)
1 x Gunner w/M249 (Lt. AP:1/AT:0)
1 x Rifleman w/M16A2

Fire Team One Charlie
1 x Fire Team Leader w/M16A2
1 x Grenadier w/M203 (Lt. AP:1/AT:0)
1 x Gunner w/M249 (Lt. AP:1/AT:0)
1 x Rifleman w/M16A2

1 x AAVTP-7 Amtrac

IRAQI MISSION

Saddam Hussein knew he could not ultimately foil the Coalition's campaign to topple his regime so he laid plans to create difficult post-war conditions in the country. This included scuttling as much infrastructure as possible, including crippling the oil industry and forcing upon the Coalition a huge, and lengthy, repair. Coupled with fledgling plans for an insurgency, it might make the Coalition's efforts in Iraq too costly in terms of both blood and treasure, forcing their withdrawal and Saddam's eventual restoration to power. At Az Zubayr oil is stored in holding tanks or transferred through a pumping station to the Al Faw Peninsula. Damage or destruction of the pumping station would cripple recovery efforts.

Use the random forces that are available to damage the facility and bloody the Marine attackers.

Iraqi Victory Points

- Damage one pumping facility with explosives: 5pts (two damaged: 10pts)
- Per Marine killed: 3pts
- Per Marine seriously wounded: 1pt
- Per Enemy Vehicle Immobilized: 2pts
- Per Enemy Vehicle Destroyed: 3pts

Iraqi Force

Iraqi Basic Attributes
Initiative Level: N/A
Confidence Level: Confident
Supply Level: Normal
Body Armor: N/A
Troop Quality/Morale: D6/D10

Ba'ath Party Death Squad
    1 x Ba'ath Party Official w/AK
    5x Saddam Fedayeen w/AK
    1 x Saddam Fedayeen w/RPG (Med. AP:2/AT:1(M))
    1 x Transport – an SUV parked near the administrative building

The Iraqi commander suffers from a lack of combat assets. Roll 1D6 and consult the chart below. Your roll determines the LONE asset available. Unless noted below, forces must set up inside the admin building.

1–3 One armed civilian guard (TQ D6, Morale D6) w/AK; 5 x Fedayeen w/AK (enter anywhere along north edge on Turn 1 in SUV – de-bus as per APC); 1 x SPG-9 recoilless rifle (Hvy. AP:3/AT:1(M); w/3 x Fedayeen crew (located in the Palm Grove)

4 Iraqi Army Infantry Conscript Rifle Section (TQ D6, Morale D6 with Ba'ath Party Official re-roll) – 1 x Leader w/AK, 7 x AK, 1 x RPK (Lt. AP:1/AT:0), 1 x RPG (Med. AP:2/AT:1(M) deployed on table in the Admin building

5 Saddam Fedayeen Cell (TQ D6, Morale D10) – 1 x Leader, 5 x AK, 1 x RPK (Lt. AP:1/AT:0), 1 x RPG (Med. AP:2/AT:1(M) (enter anywhere along north edge on Turn 1 on foot)

6 Iraqi Army Infantry Regular Rifle Section (TQ D6, Morale D8 plus Ba'ath Party re-roll) – 1 x Leader w/AK, 7 x AK, 1 x RPK (Lt. AP:1/AT:0), 1 x RPG (Med. AP:2/AT:1(M) deployed on table in the Admin building

Special Rules

Sabotaging the Turbines

Any Iraqi figure (except the civilian guard) may attempt

US Marines take cover behind a AAVTP-7 track

USMC AH-1W SUPER COBRA IN IRAQ, 2003

to set a crude explosive charge in one of the pumping stations. Each turn that a figure or unit remains in one of the two pump houses, stationary and not engaging in any offensive or defensive actions (including reactions in Rounds of Fire), and unaffected by an adverse morale result (non-Shaken), the Iraqi player may make a TQ check. If passed, the explosives are set to detonate in three turns unless disarmed by any Marine remaining stationary in the pumping station for one turn by passing a TQ check.

BREACHING

Marines must breach the external fence or the locked gate to gain entry. The AAV can be used to mechanically breach an entry point or the riflemen may set a small breaching charge (C4 or simply det-cord) by spending a turn within 1" of the wire or gate. On the next turn, the Marine player must roll a successful TQ roll to ensure the charge detonates and the breach is accomplished. If successful, the Marines can move and fire through the breach on that turn as desired. If the TQ roll is failed, the Marines may re-try each turn until accomplished (Marines may react to Rounds of Fire but not initiate offensive fires while laying the charge).

BA'ATH PARTY RE-ROLL

While the Ba'ath Party leader is alive and on table, the conscript or regular Iraqi troops may re-roll any failed morale rolls once per turn due to the institutional fear of the Ba'ath death squads. The Fedayeen do not receive this re-roll.

COBRAS!

On Turn 3 onward, the Marine commander may attempt to call in the orbiting AH-1W "Whisky" Cobra to provide close air support. Use standard TAC rules to resolve. The Cobra cannot fire upon targets in either pump house due to fear of destroying them.

A USMC COBRA ENGAGING GROUND TARGETS

Anti-Tank RPG Warheads

Each time an RPG is fired, roll 1D6. If Iraqi regular forces, a roll of 4–6 indicates an AT RPG (Hvy. AP:3/AT:2(M). If Fedayeen or foreign jihadists, a 5–6 indicates an AT RPG.

Buildings

All buildings are rated at 6D8 and provide Solid Cover. They have not been reinforced.

Optional Rules

Optional Forces

The following optional forces are provided to add to replay value of this scenario- these forces are completely hypothetical however could have plausibly deployed in defense of the pumping station. If the T-55 and BMPs are rolled add a Weapons Team of two Marines with M16A2s and a Javelin ATGM to the Marine starting forces.

Roll 1D6

1–4 1 x T-55 Tank (stats as Iraqi regulars above) enters from anywhere along north edge on Turn 2

5–6 1 x T-55 AND 2 x BMP-1s each mounting six Iraqi regular infantry (stats as Iraqi regulars above) enter anywhere along north edge on Turn 3

SCENARIO 2: UMM QASR

Umm Qasr, March 22

Elements of the 15th Marine Expeditionary Unit (Special Operations Capable) entered the port city of Umm Qasr after British Royal Marine Commando units passed through at the start of combat operations. The Marines were to secure the port facilities for the arrival of humanitarian aid. Iraqi resistance was initially light, but stiffened considerably on the second day of operations. March 22 dawned with Marine patrols working to locate Fedayeen forces in the city. At an administration building near the harbor, a patrol got into a small firefight that quickly became an intense gun battle as Marines sought to surround and eliminate the enemy threat.

Scenario Information

Duration of Game: 8 Turns

Initiative: USMC has Initiative for duration of game

Special Conditions:

- Fedayeen are Irregulars – this is an Asymmetric Engagement.
- Air Defense Environment: Light Air Defense

Fog of War: Generated normally by Reaction Tests

Table Size: 2' x 2'

USMC Mission

Fanatical Saddam Fedayeen militias have been bottled up near the port facility. A sizeable force of these irregulars has taken up positions in and around a key administrative building. They must be eliminated quickly to allow the port facility to be secured. It is vital that logistics materials begin flowing into Umm Qasr as quickly as possible, but

Historical Outcome

Iraqi resistance was so heavy that Javelin anti-tank teams and M1A1 Abrams main battle tanks eventually joined the fight to support the Marine grunts. The Javelins contributed significantly but the tanks drew such a heavy barrage of RPG fire that they were forced to pull back. Ultimately, Coalition strike aircraft appeared overhead and the Marine riflemen eased back to watch the effect of the airstrikes. After two JDAMs were dropped, resistance crumbled and the Marines were able to police up a number of prisoners. In the intense fighting, one Marine was killed.

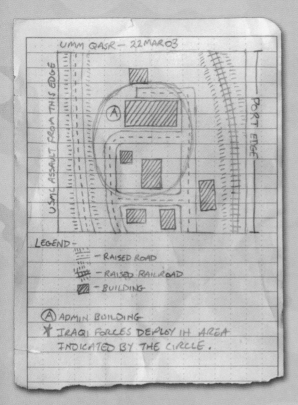

USMC casualties and damage to the harbor facilities must be kept to an absolute minimum. Armored support is inbound however most of the coming battle will be fought by the Marine rifleman.

USMC forces deploy from the western table edge on first turn.

USMC Victory Points

- Per Fedayeen Cell rendered combat ineffective (all KIA or WIA): 2pts
- No Fedayeen left on board at end of Turn 8: 3pts
- No infrastructure damage caused: 3pts

USMC Force
USMC Basic Attributes
Initiative Level: D8
Confidence Level: High

Supply Level: Normal
Body Armor: Standard (1D)
Troop Quality/Morale: D8/D10

USMC Rifle Squad One
1 x Squad Leader w/M16A2

Fire Team One Alpha
1 x Fire Team Leader w/M16A2
1 x Grenadier w/M203 (Lt. AP:1/AT:0)
1 x Gunner w/M249 (Lt. AP:1/AT:0)
1 x Rifleman w/M16A2

Fire Team One Bravo
1 x Fire Team Leader w/M16A2
1 x Grenadier w/M203 (Lt. AP:1/AT:0)
1 x Gunner w/M249 (Lt. AP:1/AT:0)
1 x Rifleman w/M16A2

Fire Team One Charlie
1 x Fire Team Leader w/M16A2
1 x Grenadier w/M203 (Lt. AP:1/AT:0)
1 x Gunner w/M249 (Lt. AP:1/AT:0)
1 x Rifleman w/M16A2

US Marines close with Fedayeen at Umm Qasr

US MARINES USING CARGO CONTAINER FOR COVER AND CONCEALMENT. (PHOTO BY PIERS BRAND, FIGURES BY ELHEIM MINIATURES)

USMC Rifle Squad Two
1 x Squad Leader w/M16A2

Fire Team Two Alpha
1 x Fire Team Leader w/M16A2
1 x Grenadier w/M203 (Lt. AP:1/AT:0)
1 x Gunner w/M249 (Lt. AP:1/AT:0)
1 x Rifleman w/M16A2

Fire Team Two Bravo
1 x Fire Team Leader w/M16A2
1 x Grenadier w/M203 (Lt. AP:1/AT:0)
1 x Gunner w/M249 (Lt. AP:1/AT:0)
1 x Rifleman w/M16A2

Fire Team Two Charlie
1 x Fire Team Leader w/M16A2
1 x Grenadier w/M203 (Lt. AP:1/AT:0)
1 x Gunner w/M249 (Lt. AP:1/AT:0)
1 x Rifleman w/M16A2

USMC M240G Weapons Team
1 x Gunner w/M240G (Med. AP:2/AT:0)
1 x Assistant Gunner w/M16A2

USMC Tank Element (Arrives on Turn 4)
1 x M1A1 HA MBT (starts game un-buttoned)

IRAQI MISSION

Iraqi forces in Umm Qasr were initially surprised by the British Royal Marine Commandos passing through the city, but became better organized and were able to put up some stiffer resistance when Marines of 15th MEU (SOC) later entered the city to secure the harbor facilities. The Iraqi leadership was fully aware of the value in giving the Coalition a bloody nose in one of the first cities entered and deployed a significant number of Uday Hussein's paramilitary irregulars, the Saddam Fedayeen, in Umm Qasr.

One such force operated out of an administration building close to the port facilities, directly threatening the security of a port vital to flow of logistics to Coalition forces. Fedayeen fighters were prepared to sell their lives in a tough battle with Marines and proved it in the fight that followed. The administration building must be held at all costs. A Fedayeen presence there prevents the invaders from using the harbor to their full advantage.

USMC M1-A1 MBT

Iraqi forces may deploy anywhere within the area circled on the map and are considered Hidden until they fire or are Spotted by USMC elements. They must deploy at least one cell in the administration building.

IRAQI VICTORY POINTS

- Per Marine killed: 3pts
- Per Marine seriously wounded: 1pt
- Per Enemy Vehicle Immobilized: 2pts
- Per Enemy Vehicle Destroyed: 3pts
- Any Fedayeen left on board at end of Turn 8: 3pts

IRAQI FORCE

Iraqi Basic Attributes

Initiative Level: N/A

Confidence Level: High

Supply Level: Normal

Body Armor: N/A

Troop Quality/Morale: D6/D10

Fedayeen Cell 1

2 x Fedayeen leader w/AK

2 x Gunners w/RPG (Med. AP:2/AT:1(M)

6 x Irregulars w/AK

USMC FIRETEAM, UMM QASR, IRAQ. (PHOTO BY PIERS BRAND, FIGURES BY ELHEIM MINIATURES)

Fedayeen Cell 2

1 x Fedayeen leader w/AK

1 x Gunner w/RPG (Med. AP:2/AT:1(M)

3 x Irregulars w/AK

Fedayeen Cell 3

1 x Fedayeen leader w/AK

1 x Gunner w/RPG (Med. AP:2/AT:1(M)

1 x Gunner w/RPK (Lt. AP:1/AT:0)

4 x Irregulars w/AK

Fedayeen Cell 4

1 x Fedayeen leader w/AK

2 x Gunners w/RPG (Med. AP:2/AT:1(M)

4 x Irregulars w/AK

Fedayeen Cell 5

1 x Fedayeen leader w/AK

1 x Gunner w/RPG (Med. AP:2/AT:1(M)

1 x Gunner w/PKM (Med. AP:2/AT:0)

5 x Irregulars w/AK

Fedayeen DShK HMG (Dushka)

3 x Crew w/AK

1 x DShK HMG (Hvy. AP:3/AT:1(L)

US MARINE, IRAQ, 2003

SPECIAL RULES

CHECK YOUR FIRE!

Any fire from any US weapon system heavier than a 40mm grenade (weapons such as the M203, Abrams .50 or COAX MG) towards the harbor edge of the table has a chance to damage or destroy harbor infrastructure. Each time such a weapon is fired towards the harbor edge the firing unit must make a Troop Quality check to avoid causing such collateral damage to infrastructure. If the check is failed, the harbor has been damaged and the Iraqi force receives 3 Victory Points each time this occurs.

BERMS AND IN COVER

Both the berm at the edge of the raised road running north to south (6" in from table edge on a 4x4) and the opposite raised railroad provide an In Cover bonus (+1d) for any deployed forces on the side facing the respective board edge.

BUILDINGS

All buildings are rated at 6D8 and provide Solid Cover. They have not been reinforced.

ANTI-TANK RPG WARHEADS

Each time an RPG is fired, roll 1D6. If Iraqi regular forces, a roll of 4–6 indicates an AT RPG (Hvy. AP:3/AT:2(M). If Fedayeen or foreign jihadists, a 5–6 indicates an AT RPG.

SCENARIO 3: CAAT FIGHT NEAR AN NASIRIYA

Near An Nasiriya, March 23

The 1st Battalion of the 2nd Marine Regiment (1/2) was tasked to secure the Euphrates River and Saddam Canal bridges on An Nasiriya's east side. Seizure of these bridges would provide the 1st Marine Regiment Combat Team (RCT-1) with a more direct drive to Baghdad rather than following RCT-5 and RCT-7's route to the south west. With Combined Anti-Armor Teams (CAAT) screening their advance, 1/2 Marines drove on towards the bridges with the M1A1s of Team Tank in support. As the CAAT entered the outskirts of An Nasiriya, the HMMWVs came under fire from machine gun and mortar positions and numerous black-clad Fedayeen fighters.

HISTORICAL OUTCOME

The firepower of the CAATs and Team Tank were simply too much for the defenders who put up a brief but heavy fight. The departure of Team Tank to rescue survivors of the ill-fated Army 507th Maintenance Company gave the Iraqis heart, but Marine riflemen of Bravo Company dismounted from their Amtracs and overran them, allowing the CAATs to continue their advance toward the bridges.

SCENARIO INFORMATION

Duration of Game: 8 Turns
Initiative: USMC for first two turns
Special Conditions:

- Fedayeen are Irregulars
- Air Defense Environment: Light Air Defense

Fog of War: Generated normally by Reaction Tests
Table Size: 3' x 6'

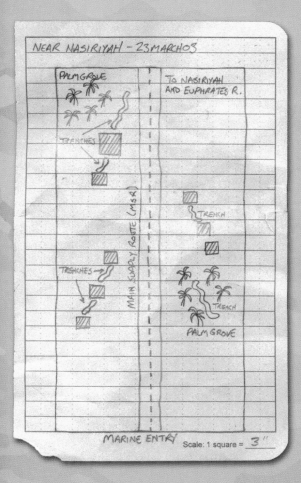

NEAR NASIRIYAH - 23MARCH03

PALMGROVE

TO NASIRIYAH AND EUPHRATES R.

TRENCHES

MAIN SUPPLY ROUTE (MSR)

TRENCH

TRENCHES

TRENCH

PALM GROVE

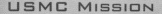

MARINE ENTRY   Scale: 1 square = 3"

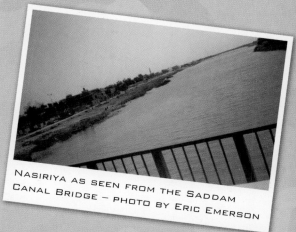

NASIRIYA AS SEEN FROM THE SADDAM CANAL BRIDGE – PHOTO BY ERIC EMERSON

USMC Force

USMC Basic Attributes
Initiative Level: D8
Confidence Level: High
Supply Level: Normal
Body Armor: Standard (1D)
Troop Quality/Morale: D8/D10

USMC Rifle Platoon
Platoon HQ (mounted in AAV with Squad One)
1 x Lieutenant w/M16A2 (Platoon leader)
1 x "Gunny" Sergeant w/M16A2 (Platoon Sergeant)
1 x RTO w/M16A2
1 x Navy Corpsman w/M16A2

USMC Mission

Advance towards An Nasiriya and neutralize any significant enemy forces that might hinder the drive for the critical bridges there. The Marines deploy with the CAAT in the lead followed by the armor of Team Tank and finally the riflemen in their AAVs.

USMC Victory Points

- Each M1A1 tank that exits north table edge: 3pts
- Each CAAT HMMWV or AAV that exits north table edge: 2pts
- No USMC KIA or POW at end of Turn 8: 5pts

A TYPICAL USMC CAAT HUMVEE

A CAAT Team Humvee puts paid to an Iraqi T-55 MBT. (Photo by Piers Brand, T-55 by Britannia Models, Humvee by Dragon Models)

USMC Rifle Squad One
1 x Squad Leader w/M16A2

Fire Team One Alpha
1 x Fire Team Leader w/M16A2
1 x Grenadier w/M203 (Lt. AP:1/AT:0)
1 x Gunner w/M249 (Lt. AP:1/AT:0)
1 x Rifleman w/M16A2

Fire Team One Bravo
1 x Fire Team Leader w/M16A2
1 x Grenadier w/M203 (Lt. AP:1/AT:0)
1 x Gunner w/M249 (Lt. AP:1/AT:0)
1 x Rifleman w/M16A2

Fire Team One Charlie
1 x Fire Team Leader w/M16A2
1 x Grenadier w/M203 (Lt. AP:1/AT:0)
1 x Gunner w/M249 (Lt. AP:1/AT:0)
1 x Rifleman w/M16A2

1 x AAVTP-7 Amtrac

USMC Rifle Squad Two (mounted in second AAV)
1 x Squad Leader w/M16A2

Fire Team Two Alpha
1 x Fire Team Leader w/M16A2
1 x Grenadier w/M203 (Lt. AP:1/AT:0)
1 x Gunner w/M249 (Lt. AP:1/AT:0)
1 x Rifleman w/M16A2

Fire Team Two Bravo
1 x Fire Team Leader w/M16A2
1 x Grenadier w/M203 (Lt. AP:1/AT:0)
1 x Gunner w/M249 (Lt. AP:1/AT:0)
1 x Rifleman w/M16A2

Fire Team Two Charlie
1 x Fire Team Leader w/M16A2

USMC AAVTP-7 kicking up dust outside An Nasiriya

1 x Grenadier w/M203 (Lt. AP:1/AT:0)
1 x Gunner w/M249 (Lt. AP:1/AT:0)
1 x Rifleman w/M16A2

1 x AAVTP-7 Amtrac

USMC CAAT Team
1 x HMMWV w/TOW Launcher (SACLOS launcher, Hvy. Support, AP:4/AT:4(H), negates ERA)
1 x HMMWV w/M2HB .50 (Hvy. AP:4/AT:1(L))

USMC 'Team Tank' Element
2 x M1A1 MBT

USMC, AN NASIRIYAH, 2003

IRAQI MISSION

An Nasiriya was a focal point of Saddam's early planning for the defense of Iraq. He knew that Coalition forces would have to accomplish toppling his regime as rapidly as possible before either a UN resolution or increasing casualties forced the Coalition to cease their offensive. However if he were to use natural obstacles to his benefit, he could lengthen the war and work at undermining Coalition or UN resolve.

In order to lengthen the conflict, he placed large numbers of Saddam Fedayeen and foreign fighters near An Nasiriya to bolster the defenses of the Iraqi

11th Division. Their defense was centered around two bridges spanning the Euphrates River and the Saddam Canal on the east side of An Nasiriya. The bridges served as a natural choke point and the soft ground around them might provide a natural defense. Therefore, a stiff defense near and at the bridges could produce a major Coalition setback.

Iraqi forces must defend the approaches to the bridges at An Nasiriya. Attack the Marines as they advance down the highway and prevent them from getting to the bridges.

IRAQI REPUBLICAN GUARD PASS A DISABLED "SHILKA" ADA VEHICLE. (PHOTO BY PIERS BRAND, FIGURES BY ELHEIM MINIATURES, SHILKA BY S&S MODELS)

IRAQI VICTORY POINTS

- No M1A1 tanks exit north board edge: 3pts
- Per Marine killed: 3pts
- Per Marine seriously wounded: 1pt
- Per Enemy Vehicle Immobilized: 2pts
- Per Enemy Vehicle Destroyed: 3pts
- At least one Iraqi unit remains on board unpinned/un-pulled back at end of Turn 8: 5pts

IRAQI FORCE

Iraqi Attributes
Initiative Level: D6
Confidence Level: Confident
Supply Level: Normal

A DESTROYED M1A1 MBT

Body Armor: N/A
Troop Quality/Morale: Varies by Unit – See below.

Under Strength Iraqi Regular Army Platoon
(TQ/Morale: D6/D8) (may deploy in any of the buildings or trench lines marked on the map)
1 x Iraqi Army 11th Infantry Regular Officer w/AK

Infantry Section One
6 x riflemen w/AKs
1 x Gunner w/RPK (Lt. AP:1/AT:0)
1 x Gunner w/RPG (Med. AP:2/AT:1(M)

Infantry Section Two
4 x riflemen w/AKs
1 x Gunner w/RPK (Lt. AP:1/AT:0)
1 x Gunner w/RPG (Med. AP:2/AT:1(M)

Infantry Section Three
4 x riflemen w/AKs
1 x Gunner w/RPK (Lt. AP:1/AT:0)
1 x Gunner w/RPG (Med. AP:2/AT:1(M)

Iraqi Regular Army PKM GPMG Team

(TQ/Morale: D6/D8 – no Weapons Team bonus)

    1 x Gunner w/PKM (Med. AP:2/AT:0)

    1 x Assistant gunner w/AK

Iraqi Regular Army Medium Mortar Team

(TQ/Morale D6/D8 – no Weapons Team bonus) (may deploy in any of the palm groves marked on the map)

    1 x 82mm Medium Mortar

    3 x Mortar Crew w/AKs

Saddam Fedayeen (may deploy in any of the palm groves marked on the map)

    Fedayeen Cell One (TQ/Morale D6/D10)

    1 x Fedayeen Leader w/AK (TQ/Morale D6/D12)

    6 x Irregulars w/AKs

    2 x Gunners w/RPGs (Med. AP:2/AT:1(M))

    Fedayeen Cell Two (TQ/Morale D6/D10)

    1 x Fedayeen Leader w/AK (TQ/Morale D6/D12)

    5 x Irregulars w/AKs

    1 x Gunner w/RPK (Lt. AP:1/AT:0)

    1 x Gunner w/RPG (Med. AP:2/AT:1(M))

    Fedayeen Cell Three (TQ/Morale D6/D10)

    1 x Fedayeen Leader w/AK (TQ/Morale D6/D12)

    5 x Irregulars w/AKs

    1 x Gunner w/RPD (Lt. AP:1/AT:0)

    2 x Gunners w/RPGs (Med. AP:2/AT:1(M))

SPECIAL RULES

TRENCHES AND PALM GROVES

The Iraqi trenches count as Improved Cover (+2d) and the palm groves provide a Solid Cover (+1d) cover bonus as long as fighters are within 2" of a palm.

RESCUE THE 507TH

The two M1A1 tanks from Team Tank depart on Turn 4 to attempt to rescue the survivors from the ambushed Army logistics convoy. The tanks advance at maximum speed toward the north edge of the table engaging any targets as they leave but not slowing down- their priority is to reach the 507th, not getting into protracted contacts with Iraqi defenders.

BUILDINGS

All buildings are rated at 6D8 and provide Solid Cover. They have not been reinforced.

ANTI-TANK RPG WARHEADS

Each time an RPG is fired, roll 1D6. If Iraqi regular forces, a roll of 4-6 indicates an AT RPG (Hvy. AP:3/AT:2(M)). If Fedayeen or foreign jihadists, a 5-6 indicates an AT RPG.

OPTIONAL RULES

OPTIONAL FORCES

The following optional forces are provided to add to replay value of this scenario.

Roll 1D6

    1–3: 2 x T-55 tanks enter north edge of board on Turn 2 (TQ/Morale D8/D8)

    4–6: 2 x Fedayeen units (equipped as per Cell One above) enter from anywhere along the western board edge on Turn 3.

SCENARIO 4: THE RAILROAD BRIDGE

Outside An Nasiriya, March 23

Despite some resistance on the southeastern outskirts of the city, SSgt Schielein's CAAT, followed by the lead elements of 1st Battalion, 2nd Marine Regiment continued to close in on the Euphrates River Bridge. Pushing up the highway, CAAT came upon a railroad line with a bridge allowing the highway to cross over it. Everything seemed pretty quiet as CAAT prepared to pass over the bridge…

HISTORICAL OUTCOME

SSgt Schielein halted the CAAT on top of the railroad bridge to scan the area. This proved a fortuitous pause as they immediately spotted and engaged a number of Iraqi T-55's in prepared positions. The CAAT TOW gunners successfully destroyed all the Iraqi armor in minutes. Marine infantry dismounted and cleared out the Iraqi infantry emplaced in the palm groves and scattered buildings on the northern side of the railroad line.

SCENARIO INFORMATION

Duration of Game: 8 Turns

Initiative: USMC retains initiative until a vehicle is destroyed or immobilized. Begin testing on the next turn.

Special Conditions:
- Fedayeen are Irregulars
- Air Defense Environment: Light Air Defense

Fog of War: Determined normally by Reaction Test rolls

Table Size: 3' x 4'

USMC MISSION

Continue pushing towards the bridges at An Nasiriya and silence any threats to the safety of the column. Cobra gunships are in support and have reported engaging enemy armor. Coalition forces deploy in column on the highway with only the CAAT deploying within 6" of the southern board edge in Turn 1. The AAVs follow and deploy in Turn 2 with their infantry cargo.

USMC VICTORY POINTS

- Each Coalition vehicle that exits north table edge: 5pts
- Each T-55 destroyed: 3pts
- No USMC KIA/POW at end of Turn 8: 3pts

USMC FORCE

USMC Basic Attributes

Initiative Level: D8

Confidence Level: Confident

Body Armor: Standard (1D)
Troop Quality/Morale: D8/D10

USMC Rifle Platoon

    Platoon HQ (mounted in AAV with Squad One)
    1 x Lieutenant w/M16A2 (Platoon leader)
    1 x Staff Sergeant w/M16A2 (Platoon Sergeant)
    1 x RTO w/M16A2
    1 x Navy Corpsman w/M16A2

    USMC Rifle Squad One
    1 x Squad Leader w/M16A2

    Fire Team One Alpha
    1 x Fire Team Leader w/M16A2
    1 x Grenadier w/M203 (Lt. AP:1/AT:0)
    1 x Gunner w/M249 (Lt. AP:1/AT:0)
    1 x Rifleman w/M16A2

    Fire Team One Bravo
    1 x Fire Team Leader w/M16A2
    1 x Grenadier w/M203 (Lt. AP:1/AT:0)
    1 x Gunner w/M249 (Lt. AP:1/AT:0)
    1 x Rifleman w/M16A2

    Fire Team One Charlie
    1 x Fire Team Leader w/M16A2
    1 x Grenadier w/M203 (Lt. AP:1/AT:0)
    1 x Gunner w/M249 (Lt. AP:1/AT:0)
    1 x Rifleman w/M16A2

    1 x AAVTP-7 Amtrac

    USMC Rifle Squad Two (mounted in second AAV)
    1 x Squad Leader w/M16A2

Fire Team Two Alpha
1 x Fire Team Leader w/M16A2
1 x Grenadier w/M203 (Lt. AP:1/AT:0)
1 x Gunner w/M249 (Lt. AP:1/AT:0)
1 x Rifleman w/M16A2

Fire Team Two Bravo
1 x Fire Team Leader w/M16A2
1 x Grenadier w/M203 (Lt. AP:1/AT:0)
1 x Gunner w/M249 (Lt. AP:1/AT:0)
1 x Rifleman w/M16A2

Fire Team Two Charlie
1 x Fire Team Leader w/M16A2
1 x Grenadier w/M203 (Lt. AP:1/AT:0)
1 x Gunner w/M249 (Lt. AP:1/AT:0)
1 x Rifleman w/M16A2

1 x AAVTP-7 Amtrac

USMC CAAT Team
2 x HMMWV w/TOW Launcher (SACLOS launcher, Hvy. Support, AP:4/AT:4(H), negates ERA)
2 x HMMWV w/M2HB .50 (Hvy. AP:4/AT:1(L)

Both M2-armed HMMWVs carry a Javelin ATGM team along with the driver and gunner:

1 x Gunner w/Javelin ATGM (Fire & Forget Launcher, Hvy. AP:4/AT:4, always hits deck armor)
1 x Rifleman w/M16A2

IRAQI MISSION

Marine units are known to be somewhere to the south of the city, but no word has come from outer defenses about any enemy activity. It is thought that some fire was

AN "UP-ARMORED" CAAT HMMWV

heard further south earlier in the day. Regardless, a series of ambush positions have been prepared to greet the invaders with a hail of lead. Iraqi armor, infantry and irregular Fedayeen units are dug in and ready to deliver a staggering blow to the Marines as they close in on the bridges spanning the Euphrates River and Saddam Canal and halt their advance on An Nasiriya.

IRAQI VICTORY POINTS

- Each T-55 not destroyed at the end of Turn 8: 3pts
- At least two Iraqi units remain on board unpinned/un-pulled back at end of Turn 8: 3pts
- Per Marine killed: 3pts
- Per Marine seriously wounded: 1pt
- Per Enemy Vehicle Immobilized: 2pts
- Per Enemy Vehicle Destroyed: 3pts

IRAQI FORCE

Iraqi Attributes

Initiative Level: D6

Confidence Level: Confident

Supply Level: Normal

Body Armor: N/A

Troop Quality/Morale: Varies by Unit – see below and use Asymmetric Command rules for the Fedayeen.

Iraqi Regular Army Platoon

(TQ/Morale: D6/D8 – may deploy in any of the palm groves north of the railroad or revetments unoccupied by tanks marked on the map)

    1 x Iraqi Army 11th Infantry Regular Officer w/AK

Infantry Section One

6 x riflemen w/AKs

1 x Gunner w/RPK (Lt. AP:1/AT:0)

1 x Gunner w/RPG (Med. AP:2/AT:1(M))

Infantry Section Two

6 x riflemen w/AKs

1 x Gunner w/RPK (Lt. AP:1/AT:0)

1 x Gunner w/RPG (Med. AP:2/AT:1(M))

IRAQI REPUBLICAN GUARD T-55 MBTs ON THE MOVE. (PHOTO BY PIERS BRAND, FIGURES BY BRITANNIA MODELS)

Infantry Section Three

6 x riflemen w/AKs

1 x Gunner w/RPK (Lt. AP:1/AT:0)

1 x Gunner w/RPG (Med. AP:2/AT:1(M)

Iraqi Regular Army PKM Teams

(TQ/Morale: D6/D8- no Weapons Team bonus – may deploy in any of the palm groves north of the railroad or revetments unoccupied by tanks marked on the map)

PKM Team One

1 x Gunner w/PKM (Med. AP:2/AT:0)

1 x Assistant gunner w/AK

PKM Team Two

1 x Gunner w/PKM (Med. AP:2/AT:0)

1 x Assistant gunner w/AK

Fedayeen

(TQ/Morale D6/D10 – may deploy Hidden in any of the buildings)

Fedayeen Cell One

1 x Fedayeen leader w/AK

2 x Gunners w/RPG (Med. AP:2/AT:1(M)

6 x Irregulars w/AK

Fedayeen Cell Two

1 x Fedayeen leader w/AK

2 x Gunner w/RPG (Med. AP:2/AT:1(M)

3 x Irregulars w/AK

Fedayeen Cell Three

1 x Fedayeen leader w/AK

2 x Gunner w/RPG (Med. AP:2/AT:1(M)

1 x Gunner w/RPK (Lt. AP:1/AT:0)

4 x Irregulars w/AK

Fedayeen Recoilless Rifle

(must deploy Hidden in the palm grove west of the buildings)

1 x Fedayeen leader w/AK

2 x Crew w/AK

1 x SPG-9 73mm Recoilless Rifle (Hvy. AP:3/AT:2(L)

Tank Platoon (TQ/Morale D6/D8)

Two tanks may start the game under the north side of the railroad bridge or in the armor revetments marked on the map. The remainder of the tanks must begin the game placed in the revetments.

4 x T-55 Tanks

SPECIAL RULES

REVETMENTS, BUILDINGS AND PALM GROVES

The Iraqi revetments count as Improved Cover (+2D) and the palm groves provide a Solid Cover (+1D) cover bonus as long as fighters are within 2" of a palm.

BUILDINGS

All buildings are rated at 6D8 and provide Solid Cover. They have not been reinforced.

ANTI-TANK RPG WARHEADS

Each time an RPG is fired, roll 1D6. If Iraqi regular forces, a roll of 4-6 indicates an AT RPG (Hvy. AP:3/AT:2(M). If Fedayeen or foreign jihadists, a 5-6 indicates an AT RPG.

SCENARIO 5: AMBUSH ALLEY

An Nasiriya, March 23

After crossing the Southern Euphrates Bridge, Charlie Company, 1st Battalion, 2nd Marines advanced toward their next objective, the Northern Saddam Canal Bridge. Their

IRAQI T-55 TANK IN HASTILY DUG REVETMENT

This scenario has been reduced in size for game-play and simulates the lead elements of Charlie Company entering Ambush Alley.

Scenario Information

Duration of Game: 6 Turns

Initiative: USMC has Initiative for duration of game

Special Conditions:

- Fedayeen are Irregulars – this is an Asymmetric Engagement.
- Air Defense Environment: Light Air Defense

Fog of War: Determined normally by Reaction Test rolls

Table Size: 2' x 3'

tank support reluctantly were forced to stop at the Euphrates as they feared the bridge would not support the seventy ton M1A1s and they wanted to ensure Charlie Company in their Amtracs crossed safely before attempting the crossing. Charlie Company passed through Alpha Company's bridgehead position on the northern bank and advanced toward the Northern Saddam Canal, straight down the infamous 4.6km main supply route which would become known as Ambush Alley.

Historical Outcome

As Charlie Company left the dismounted Alpha, they were engaged immediately by heavy small arms and RPG fire from Saddam Fedayeen hidden in buildings on either side of the four-lane Ambush Alley. The company managed to punch through, losing an AAV in the process and finally crossing the Northern Saddam Canal Bridge where they stopped and awaited their tank support. Tragically, they were mistakenly engaged by a pair of Air National Guard A-10 Warthogs, killing a number of Marines and destroying several AAVs.

AMBUSH ALLEY – 23 MAR '03

NORTHERN SADDAM CANAL BRIDGE

MARINE ENTRY POINT

Scale: 1 square = 2"

USMC Mission

Charlie Company must advance through Ambush Alley and reach the Northern Saddam Canal Bridge. You must attempt to reach the Bridge with minimal casualties and loss of Marine vehicles while avoiding getting caught in Ambush Alley.

All Marine vehicles enter the board directly into Ambush Alley in Turn 1.

USMC Victory Points

- Each Coalition vehicle that exits north table edge: 5pts
- No USMC KIA/POW at end of Turn 6: 3pts

USMC Force

USMC Basic Attributes

Initiative Level: D8
Confidence Level: Confident
Supply Level: Normal
Body Armor: Standard (1D)
Troop Quality/Morale: D8/D10

USMC Rifle Squad One (mounted in first AAV)
1 x Squad Leader w/M16A2

Fire Team One Alpha
1 x Fire Team Leader w/M16A2
1 x Grenadier w/M203 (Lt. AP:1/AT:0)
1 x Gunner w/M249 (Lt. AP:1/AT:0)
1 x Rifleman w/M16A2

Fire Team One Bravo
1 x Fire Team Leader w/M16A2
1 x Grenadier w/M203 (Lt. AP:1/AT:0)
1 x Gunner w/M249 (Lt. AP:1/AT:0)
1 x Rifleman w/M16A2

Fire Team One Charlie
1 x Fire Team Leader w/M16A2
1 x Grenadier w/M203 (Lt. AP:1/AT:0)
1 x Gunner w/M249 (Lt. AP:1/AT:0)
1 x Rifleman w/M16A2

1 x AAVTP-7 Amtrac

USMC Rifle Squad Two (mounted in second AAV)
1 x Squad Leader w/M16A2

Fire Team Two Alpha
1 x Fire Team Leader w/M16A2
1 x Grenadier w/M203 (Lt. AP:1/AT:0)
1 x Gunner w/M249 (Lt. AP:1/AT:0)
1 x Rifleman w/M16A2

Fire Team Two Bravo
1 x Fire Team Leader w/M16A2
1 x Grenadier w/M203 (Lt. AP:1/AT:0)
1 x Gunner w/M249 (Lt. AP:1/AT:0)
1 x Rifleman w/M16A2

US MARINES CLEAR AN ALLEY IN NASIRIYA. (PHOTO BY JUSTIN POWLES, FIGURES BY PETER PIG)

Fire Team Two Charlie
1 x Fire Team Leader w/M16A2
1 x Grenadier w/M203 (Lt. AP:1/AT:0)
1 x Gunner w/M249 (Lt. AP:1/AT:0)
1 x Rifleman w/M16A2

1 x AAVTP-7 Amtrac

USMC Rifle Squad Three (mounted in third AAV)
1 x Squad Leader w/M16A2

Fire Team Three Alpha
1 x Fire Team Leader w/M16A2
1 x Grenadier w/M203 (Lt. AP:1/AT:0)
1 x Gunner w/M249 (Lt. AP:1/AT:0)
1 x Rifleman w/M16A2

Fire Team Three Bravo
1 x Fire Team Leader w/M16A2
1 x Grenadier w/M203 (Lt. AP:1/AT:0)
1 x Gunner w/M249 (Lt. AP:1/AT:0)
1 x Rifleman w/M16A2

Fire Team Three Charlie
1 x Fire Team Leader w/M16A2
1 x Grenadier w/M203 (Lt. AP:1/AT:0)
1 x Gunner w/M249 (Lt. AP:1/AT:0)
1 x Rifleman w/M16A2

1 x AAVTP-7 Amtrac

Iraqi Mission

The Saddam Fedayeen must attempt to stop the Americans reaching the Northern Saddam Canal Bridge which will allow them a straight run north toward the capital. Disable their vehicles and force them to call off their advance.

Iraqi Victory Points

Per Marine killed: 3pts
Per Marine seriously wounded: 1pt
Per Enemy Vehicle Immobilized: 2pts
Per Enemy Vehicle Destroyed: 3pts

Iraqi Force

Iraqi Basic Attributes
Initiative Level: D6
Confidence Level: Confident
Supply Level: Normal
Body Armor: N/A
Troop Quality/Morale: D6/D10

Initial Fedayeen Force
(TQ/Morale D6/D10 – all deploy initially Hidden in any building)

Fedayeen Cell One
1 x Fedayeen leader w/AK
1 x Gunners w/RPG (Med. AP:2/AT:1(M))
4 x Irregulars w/AK

Fedayeen Cell Two
1 x Fedayeen leader w/AK
2 x Gunners w/RPG (Med. AP:2/AT:1(M))
4 x Irregulars w/AK

Fedayeen Cell Three
1 x Fedayeen leader w/AK
2 x Gunners w/RPG (Med. AP:2/AT:1(M))
1 x Gunner w/RPK (Lt. AP:1/AT:0)
5 x Irregulars w/AK

Fedayeen Cell Four
1 x Fedayeen leader w/AK
1 x Gunner w/RPG (Med. AP:2/AT:1(M))
6 x Irregulars w/AK

Fedayeen Cell Five

1 x Fedayeen leader w/AK

1 x Gunner w/RPG (Med. AP:2/AT:1(M))

4 x Irregulars w/AK

Reinforcements

On Turn 2 and every turn thereafter, reinforcements automatically arrive for the Saddam Fedayeen and may be placed up to 6" from a random board edge (roll 1D6, 1–3 West, 4–6 East).

IRAQI FEDAYEEN IN INFAMOUS "VADER" HELMETS. (PHOTO BY PIERS BRAND, FIGURES BY ELHEIM MINIATURES)

REINFORCEMENT TABLE

Roll 1D10:
(ALL STATS TQ/MORALE D6/D10)

1.	4 x Irregulars w/AK, 1 x Leader w/AK
2.	4 x Irregulars w/AK, 1 x Leader w/AK, 1 x Gunner w/Med. Support
3.	1 x Gunner w/Med. Support, 1 x Irregular w/AK
4.	1 x SVD Dragunov sniper, 1 x Irregular w/AK
5.	1 x Gunner w/PKM (Med. AP:2/AT:0), 1 x Irregular w/AK
6.	1 x 60mm light mortar with 1 x crew and 1 x spotter with AK
7.	6 x Irregulars w/AK, 1 x Leader w/AK, 1 x Gunner w/Med. Support
8.	6 x Irregulars w/AK, 1 x Leader w/AK, 1 x Gunner w/Med. Support, 1 x RPK gunner
9.	1 x DShK HMG (Hvy. AP:3/AT:1(L) with 3 x crew
10.	Off Table 82mm Medium Mortar Barrage Medium Support – Roll 1D6 for type:

Medium Support – Roll 1D6 for type:
1:      AT RPG (Hvy. AP:3/AT:2(M)
2-4:   RPG (Med. AP:2/AT:1(M)
5-6:   PKM MG (Med. AP:2/AT:0)

SPECIAL RULES

BUILDINGS

All buildings are rated at 6D8 and provide Solid Cover. They have not been reinforced.

OUT OF CONTACT MOVEMENT

The Fedayeen may use Out of Contact Movement.

BLUE ON BLUE!

On Turns 4 and 5, there is a chance of a blue on blue engagement of the Marines by a pair of orbiting A-10 Warthog ground attack aircraft. At the end of each turn, roll a D8 TQ check. If failed, an A-10 will strafe a random AAV with its 30mm cannon (AP:6/AT:4(M) vs. Deck). If the TQ check is failed on both turns, one of the A-10s will launch a Maverick ATGM (AP:4/AT:5(H) vs. Deck) against a random AAV at the beginning of Turn 6.

If all US units are off-board by the beginning of Turns 4, 5, or 6, then no Blue on Blue attack is resolved for that turn.

AN IRAQI REGULAR ARMY SNIPER TEAM SCRAMBLES TO FIND A GOOD SHOOTING POSITION. (PHOTO BY PIERS BRAND, FIGURES BY ELHEIM MINIATURES)

MORTARS

On Turns 5 and 6, a battery of off-board 60mm mortars may be used in support of Charlie Company. Use standard mortar rules (AP:3/AT:0 (3" radius). Remember to account for Danger Close fires.

MARINE COUNTER BATTERY

The Marines have access to off-table counter battery radar and supporting artillery. Apply the Counter Battery rules as described in *Force on Force*.

ANTI-TANK RPG WARHEADS

Each time an RPG is fired, roll 1D6. If Iraqi regular forces, a roll of 4–6 indicates an AT RPG (Hvy. AP:3/AT:2(M). If Fedayeen or foreign jihadists, a 5–6 indicates an AT RPG.

OPTIONAL RULES

AMBIENT FIRE

As per the Ambient Fire rules against helicopters, you may introduce Ambient Fire against each element in the Charlie Company advance to simulate the relentless fire encountered in Ambush Alley. Each turn, the Iraqi player may roll a 3D8 attack against each vehicle and dismounted infantry element on the board – this simulates both small arms and RPG fire – in addition to all normal firing. This can prove to be quite lethal and is only recommended once you have played the basic scenario at least once.

SCENARIO 6: THE ALAMO

An Nasiriya, March 23

Charlie Company, 1st Battalion, 2nd Marines attack on the Saddam Canal Bridge met stiff resistance. Mounting casualties required urgent medical evacuation however the HLZs for the medevac helicopters were under heavy Iraqi fire. A ground evacuation with five Amtracs was organized to move the Marine casualties back through the city. This meant a run back through Ambush Alley. Before the column reached Alpha Company lines, Iraqi RPGs hit several Amtracs, disabling one. The Marines bailed out and sheltered in a 2-story house while the remainder of the column managed to withdraw relatively unscathed. For the next three hours, these 25 Marines conducted a modern day "Rorke's Drift", reminiscent of the plight of Task Force Ranger in Mogadishu in 1993.

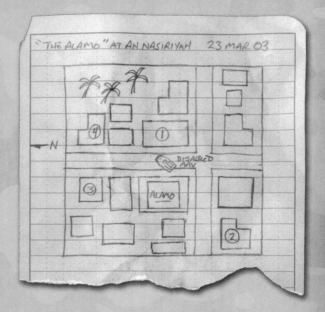

SCENARIO INFORMATION

Duration of Game: 8 Turns

Initiative: US for duration of game

Special Conditions:

- Fedayeen are Irregulars – this is an Asymmetric Engagement.
- Air Defense Environment: Light Air Defense

Fog of War: Determined normally by Reaction Test rolls

Table Size: 2' x 2'

- **1–4:** Fedayeen Cells
- **Alamo:** Location of US Marines

USMC Mission

Your unit is cut off and must await rescue in a house near the disabled Amtrac. The Amtrac hit by hostile fire rests in the street outside the house. You must keep from being overrun and prevent Iraqi forces from looting the Amtrac while working to keep any seriously wounded personnel alive. Additionally, you must recover ammunition from the vehicle as you are exhausting the basic load carried by the Marine riflemen.

MARINES TAKE TO THE ROOFTOPS TO SECURE THEIR STRONGPOINT. (PHOTO BY JUSTIN POWLES, FIGURES BY PETER PIG)

USMC Victory Points

- Prevent AAV being looted: 2pts
- Prevent Alamo from being overrun (no Iraqis inside the strongpoint at any point during the game): 3pts
- USMC successfully exfiltrate with relief force by end of Turn 8: 5pts

USMC Force

USMC Basic Attributes

Initiative Level: D8
Confidence Level: Confident
Supply Level: Normal till Turn 5, then Poor
Body Armor: Standard (1D)
Troop Quality/Morale: D8/D10

USMC Survivors

USMC Rifle Squad One

1 x Squad Leader w/M16A2

Fire Team One Alpha
1 x Fire Team Leader w/M16A2
1 x Grenadier w/M203 (Lt. AP:1/AT:0)

US INFANTRYMAN, BAGHDAD, 2004

1 x Gunner w/M249 (Lt. AP:1/AT:0)
1 x Rifleman w/M16A2

Fire Team One Bravo
1 x Fire Team Leader w/M16A2
1 x Grenadier w/M203 (Lt. AP:1/AT:0)
1 x Gunner w/M249 (Lt. AP:1/AT:0)
1 x Rifleman w/M16A2

Fire Team One Charlie
1 x Fire Team Leader w/M16A2
1 x Grenadier w/M203 (Lt. AP:1/AT:0)
1 x Gunner w/M249 (Lt. AP:1/AT:0)
1 x Rifleman w/M16A2

USMC Rifle Squad Two
1 x Squad Leader w/M16A2

Fire Team Two Alpha
1 x Fire Team Leader w/M16A2
1 x Grenadier w/M203 (Lt. AP:1/AT:0)
1 x Gunner w/M249 (Lt. AP:1/AT:0)
1 x Rifleman w/M16A2

IRAQI MISSION

Iraqi forces must overrun the Marines, loot the Amtrac and prevent the Marines' escape. Each objective accomplished is more propaganda for the network news and Al Jazeera. Fresh fighters will join the attack continuously. It is only a matter of time until the Marines are overrun!

IRAQI VICTORY POINTS

- Overrun the Marine position by having at least one Iraqi unit enter the building while it is occupied: 3pts
- Kill, wound or capture all Marines in the Alamo: 5pts
- Kill or capture a Marine: 1pt
- Loot the AAV: 2pts
- Each vehicle disabled/destroyed: 2pts

IRAQI FORCE

Iraqi Basic Attributes

Initiative Level: D6

Confidence Level: Confident

Supply Level: Normal

Body Armor: N/A

Troop Quality/Morale: D6/D10

Initial Fedayeen Force

Fedayeen Cell One

1 x Fedayeen leader w/AK

1 x Gunner w/RPG (Med. AP:2/AT:1(M)

5 x Irregulars w/AK

Fedayeen Cell Two

1 x Fedayeen leader w/AK

2 x Gunners w/RPG (Med. AP:2/AT:1(M)

4 x Irregulars w/AK

Fedayeen Cell Three

1 x Fedayeen leader w/AK

2 x Gunners w/RPG (Med. AP:2/AT:1(M)

1 x Gunner w/RPK (Lt. AP:1/AT:0)

5 x Irregulars w/AK

Fedayeen Cell Four

1 x Fedayeen leader w/AK

1 x Gunner w/RPG (Med. AP:2/AT:1(M)

6 x Irregulars w/AK

Reinforcements

On Turn 2 and every turn thereafter, reinforcements automatically arrive for the Saddam Fedayeen and may be placed up to 6" from a random board edge (roll 1D6, 1–2 North, 3–4 East, 5–6 West). The southern table edge is assumed to be held by nearby Marines.

REINFORCEMENT TABLE	
ROLL 1D10:	
(ALL STATS TQ/MORALE D6/D10)	
1.	4 x Irregulars w/AK, 1 x Leader w/AK
2.	4 x Irregulars w/AK, 1 x Leader w/AK, 1 x Gunner w/Med. Support
3.	1 x Gunner w/Med. Support, 1 x Irregular w/AK
4.	1 x SVD Dragunov sniper, 1 x Irregular w/AK
5.	1 x Gunner w/PKM (Med. AP:2/AT:0), 1 x Irregular w/AK
6.	1 x 60mm light mortar with 1 x crew and 1 x spotter with AK
7.	6 x Irregulars w/AK, 1 x Leader w/AK, 1 x Gunner w/Med. Support
8.	6 x Irregulars w/AK, 1 x Leader w/AK, 1 x Gunner w/Med. Support, 1 x RPK gunner
9.	1 x DShK HMG (Hvy. AP:3/AT:1(L) with 3 x crew
10.	Off Table 82mm Medium Mortar Barrage
Medium Support – Roll 1D6 for type:	
1: AT RPG (Hvy. AP:3/AT:2(M)	
2-4: RPG (Med. AP:2/AT:1(M)	
5-6: PKM MG (Med. AP:2/AT:0)	

SPECIAL RULES

THE ALAMO

Deploy the Marines in the Alamo building or within 6 inches of its walls. The Alamo is a walled compound style house with a ground and upper floor with flat roofs and parapets for cover. The Alamo building is considered Improved Cover (+2D) for purposes of cover, and 8D8 for building destruction tests. All other buildings are rated at 6D8 and provide Solid Cover. They have not been reinforced.

US FIRETEAM, BAGHDAD, 2004

USMC REINFORCEMENTS:

On Turn 2, a lone, and very lost, AAVTP-7 drives across the east/west road, engaging all targets that fire upon it or are obviously armed. It does not see the Marines in the Alamo, nor will it stop for any reason, and continues at full speed until it exits the board.

On Turn 4 one M1A1 Abrams, nicknamed 'The Black Knight', drives on from the southern edge at full speed, engaging any targets that fire upon it (Reaction Fire) or any obviously armed targets, before stopping directly outside the gates to the Alamo. The crew volunteers to remove up to four seriously wounded and any KIA.

It takes one fire team, or four Marines made up from different teams, one full turn to load up to four WIA and any KIA- this is abstracted to enhance game-play. The Abrams cannot fire its main gun while it is being loaded but can engage with coax and TC MGs. If it is not utilized for casualty evacuation, the M1A1 will retreat off board in the same manner it entered on Turn 5, firing as it goes at full speed.

On Turn 6, four standard HMMWVs, each with two crew (driver and gunner), led by Gunnery Sgt Doran (Positive Leader), appear from the south edge of the table at speed to rescue the defenders. The HMMWVs mount 2 x M2 .50, 1 x Mk19 and 1 x M240 GPMG – all are standard un-up-armored HMMWVs.

FAT LOOT

An Iraqi unit can loot the AAV by spending an entire turn in contact with the vehicle. At the end of the turn, make a Troop Quality check for the unit. Add a -1 modifier to the die roll if the unit was fired on or assaulted at any point during the turn. If the Troop Check is successful, the unit has found useful loot and gained +2 VP for the Iraqi player. If the Troop Check is unsuccessful, the unit found nothing. It can either move away on its next activation or spend another turn ransacking the AAV.

WE HAVE CASUALTIES!

At the beginning of the first turn, randomly select by die roll five Marines and mark them as lightly wounded. The fireteams the wounded men belong to suffer the Casualties penalty.

A MARINE JAVELIN TEAM PREPARES TO ENGAGE THE ENEMY FROM A ROOFTOP POSITION. (PHOTO BY PIERS BRAND, FIGURES BY ELHEIM MINIATURES)

AMMO ANXIETY!

Ammunition becomes low on Turn 5. Unless the AAV is raided for more ammunition, all fire teams become Poorly Supplied and lose a FP die until the end of the game.

Extra ammunition is stored in the disabled AAV. A Marine fire team that spends one turn in base contact can return with enough ammunition for the rest of the Marine force for the remainder of the battle (they may React but not initiate fires while collecting the ammunition). They also collect an operable Javelin CLU launcher with two missiles.

TANK OR TAXI?

Once US forces make base contact with the M1A1, the tank cannot engage targets with its main gun due to the close proximity of infantry and the risk from the concussion effects of the 120mm. Once casualties are loaded on to the tank, it cannot fire either its main gun or coax, leaving only the TC and Loader turret MGs to fire (with non-buttoned-up crew rules to apply).

There is a one turn delay for a fire team in base contact with a HMMWV or the M1A1 to load the casualties on to the vehicle.

SCOWL FOR THE CAMERA!

An al Jazeera camera man is recording the action. Place with a random Iraqi unit. Any KIAs, WIAs or prisoners taken with the camera man in LOS adds an extra VP. If he is killed by USMC fire, the Marines take a -3 to their VPs to account for the negative media coverage. Roll a TQ check when the unit he is attached to is engaged with a failure indicating he has been hit.

OUT OF CONTACT MOVEMENT

The Fedayeen may use Out of Contact Movement.

ANTI-TANK RPG WARHEADS

Each time an RPG is fired, roll 1D6. If Iraqi regular forces, a roll of 4–6 indicates an AT RPG (Hvy. AP:3/AT:2(M)). If Fedayeen or foreign jihadists, a 5–6 indicates an AT RPG.

SCENARIO 7: THE AFAK DRILL

Afak, March 23

Marine Commanding General Mattis emphasized speed and maneuver for the advance on Baghdad. The standard drill practiced by the Marines taking a series of towns and cities on the road to Baghdad, was to screen the point of advance, saturate the area with aimed fire from available assets and envelope from the open flanks. This method became known as "The Afak Drill" (or the "Oh F*ck Drill" in the laconic humor of the Marine infantryman) for its initial trial run at the city of Afak and was pioneered by Lieutenant Colonel McCoy, battalion commander of RCT-7's 3rd Battalion, 4th Marines.

RCT-7's march north to Baghdad passed through Afak located on Route 17. The RCT-7 column, led by McCoy's 3rd Battalion, 4th Marines, was tasked with breaking through Iraqi resistance in the town and moving on to Al Budayr. Deploying armor in the lead, highly mobile CAAT teams screening the flanks and infantry mounted in AAVs following the M1A1s, McCoy's Marines advanced on the defenders of Afak.

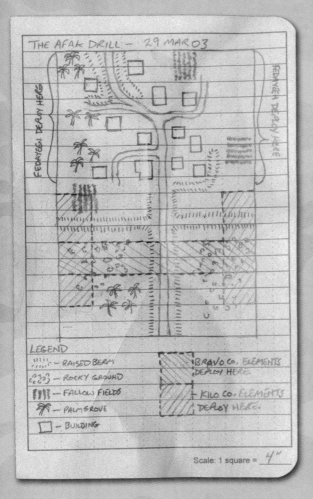

HISTORICAL OUTCOME

The Afak Drill demonstrated the inability of Iraqi forces to stand against the well-trained and coordinated Coalition forces. McCoy established a base of fire with his Bravo company and tasked Kilo, and its attached tanks, to roll in from the western flank. The Fedayeen defenders were caught completely by surprise and were engaged and broken by the advancing armor.

SCENARIO INFORMATION

Duration of Game: 8 Turns

Initiative: US for duration of game

Special Conditions:

- Fedayeen are Irregulars – this is an Asymmetric Engagement.
- Air Defense Environment: Light Air Defense

Fog of War: Determined normally by Reaction Test rolls

Table Size: 4' x 6'

USMC MISSION

The city of Afak must be taken. Per doctrine, part of the USMC force is to bring effective suppressive fires from the front while a maneuver element Abrams tanks with supporting infantry flanks the position. The town itself has one and two story buildings made of stone and brick. Dragon Eye drone intelligence confirms few people in the streets, but a lot of Fedayeen activity is noted near the Ba'ath Party headquarters.

Bravo Company elements, as the base of fire, can deploy anywhere along a line 6" from and parallel to the southern edge of the North-South berm outside of Afak. Kilo Company, with its armor in the lead followed by the dismounted infantry, can enter on either the North or South flanks of the berm within 6" in from the table edge and within 6" of the eastern edge of the berm. Kilo deploys on table in Turn 3.

USMC VICTORY POINTS

- Exit at least one rifle squad (three fire teams) off the east board edge by end of Turn eight: 5pts
- Keep Marine casualties (KIA or Serious WIA) to less than 10% of the committed force: 3pts

USMC FORCE

USMC Basic Attributes
Initiative Level: D8
Confidence Level: Confident
Supply Level: Normal
Body Armor: Standard (1D)
Troop Quality/Morale: D8/D10

Bravo Company elements
  Battalion HQ
  (Mounted in HMMWV mounting M2 .50)
  1 x Driver w/M16A2
  1 x Battalion Commander w/M16A2
  1 x Sergeant-Major w/M16A2
  1 x RTO w/M16A2

USMC Rifle Squad One (mounted in first AAV)
1 x Squad Leader w/M16A2

Fire Team One Alpha
1 x Fire Team Leader w/M16A2
1 x Grenadier w/M203 (Lt. AP:1/AT:0)
1 x Gunner w/M249 (Lt. AP:1/AT:0)
1 x Rifleman w/M16A2

Fire Team One Bravo
1 x Fire Team Leader w/M16A2
1 x Grenadier w/M203 (Lt. AP:1/AT:0)
1 x Gunner w/M249 (Lt. AP:1/AT:0)
1 x Rifleman w/M16A2

Fire Team One Charlie
1 x Fire Team Leader w/M16A2
1 x Grenadier w/M203 (Lt. AP:1/AT:0)
1 x Gunner w/M249 (Lt. AP:1/AT:0)
1 x Rifleman w/M16A2

1 x AAVTP-7 Amtrac

USMC Rifle Squad Two (mounted in second AAV)
1 x Squad Leader w/M16A2

Fire Team Two Alpha
1 x Fire Team Leader w/M16A2
1 x Grenadier w/M203 (Lt. AP:1/AT:0)
1 x Gunner w/M249 (Lt. AP:1/AT:0)
1 x Rifleman w/M16A2

Fire Team Two Bravo
1 x Fire Team Leader w/M16A2

1 x Grenadier w/M203 (Lt. AP:1/AT:0)
1 x Gunner w/M249 (Lt. AP:1/AT:0)
1 x Rifleman w/M16A2

Fire Team Two Charlie
1 x Fire Team Leader w/M16A2
1 x Grenadier w/M203 (Lt. AP:1/AT:0)
1 x Gunner w/M249 (Lt. AP:1/AT:0)
1 x Rifleman w/M16A2

1 x AAVTP-7 Amtrac

Attached Weapons Squad (mounted in second AAV)
1 x Squad Leader w/M16A2

M240G GPMG Weapon Team
1 x Gunner w/M240G (Med. AP:2/AT:0)
2 x Riflemen w/M16A2

SMAW Team
1 x Gunner w/SMAW (Med. AP:4/AT:2(H) with +1 Positive Die shift to FP when attempting to destroy a building)
1 x Rifleman w/M16A2

US INFANTRY RAID A BOMBMAKING FACILITY, BAGHDAD, 2003

Kilo Company elements
  Attached Tank Section
  2 x M1A1 Abrams

USMC Platoon Elements (Dismounted)
  USMC Rifle Squad One
  1 x Squad Leader w/M16A2

Fire Team One Alpha
1 x Fire Team Leader w/M16A2
1 x Grenadier w/M203 (Lt. AP:1/AT:0)
1 x Gunner w/M249 (Lt. AP:1/AT:0)
1 x Rifleman w/M16A2

Fire Team One Bravo
1 x Fire Team Leader w/M16A2
1 x Grenadier w/M203 (Lt. AP:1/AT:0)
1 x Gunner w/M249 (Lt. AP:1/AT:0)
1 x Rifleman w/M16A2

Fire Team One Charlie
1 x Fire Team Leader w/M16A2

US MARINES DISMOUNTING FROM AN AAV.
(PHOTO BY PIERS BRAND, FIGURES BY ELHEIM
MINIATURES, VEHICLE BY DRAGON MODELS)

1 x Grenadier w/M203 (Lt. AP:1/AT:0)
1 x Gunner w/M249 (Lt. AP:1/AT:0)
1 x Rifleman w/M16A2

USMC Rifle Squad Two
1 x Squad Leader w/M16A2

Fire Team Two Alpha
1 x Fire Team Leader w/M16A2
1 x Grenadier w/M203 (Lt. AP:1/AT:0)
1 x Gunner w/M249 (Lt. AP:1/AT:0)
1 x Rifleman w/M16A2

Fire Team Two Bravo
1 x Fire Team Leader w/M16A2
1 x Grenadier w/M203 (Lt. AP:1/AT:0)
1 x Gunner w/M249 (Lt. AP:1/AT:0)
1 x Rifleman w/M16A2

Fire Team Two Charlie
1 x Fire Team Leader w/M16A2
1 x Grenadier w/M203 (Lt. AP:1/AT:0)
1 x Gunner w/M249 (Lt. AP:1/AT:0)
1 x Rifleman w/M16A2

IRAQI MISSION

US Marines are approaching the weakly held town of Afak. It is unclear why they have diverted to the east along Highway 17 but they are approaching the defenses around the town. Our forces are scrambling to form a tougher defense to this unexpected avenue of advance. Moreover, the Iraqi leadership is desperate to garner a propaganda victory to air on the network news and are ordering desperate defense to the death everywhere.

Defend Afak to the death, making it as costly for the Marines as possible. If a victory cannot be won for the

Iraqi leadership, at least give them some fodder for the Information Minister in Baghdad. Fedayeen forces may be deployed anywhere on the board at least 6" from the eastern edge of the North-South Berm.

IRAQI VICTORY POINTS

- No Marine units exit from East edge of board: 5pts
- Each M1A1 disabled or destroyed: 3pts
- Each AAV disabled or destroyed: 2pts
- Each Marine KIA/Serious WIA or POW: 1pt

IRAQI FORCE

Iraqi Basic Attributes

Initiative Level: D6

Confidence Level: Confident

Supply Level: Normal

Body Armor: N/A

Troop Quality/Morale: D6/D10

Fedayeen/Ba'ath Party Command (TQ/Morale: D6/D12)

  1 x Fedayeen leader w/AK

  1x bodyguard w/AK

Fedayeen Technicals

  1 x Technical mounting a 12.7mm DShK (Hvy. AP:4/AT:1(L) and crewed by driver, passenger, gunner and assistant gunner (all with personal AKs)

  1 x Technical mounting a 7.62mm PKM (Med. AP:3/AT:0) and crewed by driver, passenger, gunner and assistant gunner (all with personal AKs)

Initial Fedayeen Force

(all deploy initially Hidden in any building)

  Fedayeen Cell One

  1 x Fedayeen leader w/AK

  1 x Gunner w/RPG (Med. AP:2/AT:1(M)

  6 x Irregulars w/AK

FEDAYEEN TECHNICALS. (PHOTO BY PIERS BRAND, FIGURES BY ELHEIM MINIATURES, VEHICLES BY S&S MODELS)

Fedayeen Cell Two

1 x Fedayeen leader w/AK

2 x Gunners w/RPG (Med. AP:2/AT:1(M)

5 x Irregulars w/AK

Fedayeen Cell Three

1 x Fedayeen leader w/AK

2 x Gunners w/RPG (Med. AP:2/AT:1(M)

1 x Gunner w/RPK (Lt. AP:1/AT:0)

6 x Irregulars w/AK

Fedayeen Cell Four

1 x Fedayeen leader w/AK

1 x Gunner w/RPG (Med. AP:2/AT:1(M)

6 x Irregulars w/AK

Fedayeen RPG Team One (no weapons team bonus)

1 x Gunner w/RPG with AT warheads (Hvy. AP:3/AT:2(M)

1 x Irregular w/AK

Fedayeen RPG Team Two (no weapons team bonus)

1 x Gunner w/RPG with AT warheads (Hvy. AP:3/AT:2(M)

1 x Irregular w/AK

Reinforcements

On Turn 2 and every turn thereafter, reinforcements automatically arrive for the Saddam Fedayeen and may be placed up to 6" from the eastern board edge.

REINFORCEMENT TABLE	
Roll 1D10:	
(all stats TQ/Morale D6/D10)	
1.	4 x Irregulars w/AK, 1 x Leader w/AK
2.	4 x Irregulars w/AK, 1 x Leader w/AK, 1 x Gunner w/Med. Support
3.	1 x Gunner w/Med. Support, 1 x Irregular w/AK
4.	1 x SVD Dragunov sniper, 1 x Irregular w/AK
5.	1 x Gunner w/PKM (Med. AP:2/AT:0), 1 x Irregular w/AK
6.	1 x 60mm light mortar with 1 x crew and 1 x spotter with AK
7.	6 x Irregulars w/AK, 1 x Leader w/AK, 1 x Gunner w/Med. Support
8.	6 x Irregulars w/AK, 1 x Leader w/AK, 1 x Gunner w/Med. Support, 1 x RPK gunner
9.	1 x DShK HMG (Hvy. AP:3/AT:1(L) with 3 x crew
10.	Off Table 82mm Medium Mortar Barrage
Medium Support – Roll 1D6 for type: 1: AT RPG (Hvy. AP:3/AT:2(M) 2-4: RPG (Med. AP:2/AT:1(M) 5-6: PKM MG (Med. AP:2/AT:0)	

Special Rules

Buildings

All buildings are rated at 6D8 and provide Solid Cover. They have not been reinforced.

Out of Contact Movement

The Fedayeen may use Out of Contact Movement.

Berms and In Cover

The berm across the center of the board running north to south provides an In Cover bonus (+1d) for any deployed forces on the southern side facing away from Afak.

Marine Counter Battery

The Marines have access to off-table counter battery radar and supporting artillery. On the turn immediately following an off board Iraqi indirect fire mission, the Marine player may roll a TQ opposed test against the TQ of his Iraqi counterpart with a successful roll indicating that counter battery fire has neutralized the Iraqi fire support for the remainder of a game.

Cobras!

On Turn 3 onward, the Marine commander may attempt to call in an orbiting AH-1W Cobra to provide close air support. Use standard TAC rules to resolve.

A USMC Super Cobra keeps watch over advancing Marines on the ground

ANTI-TANK RPG WARHEADS

Each time an RPG is fired, roll 1D6. If Iraqi regular forces, a roll of 4-6 indicates an AT RPG (Hvy. AP:3/AT:2(M)). If Fedayeen or foreign jihadists, a 5-6 indicates an AT RPG.

SCENARIO 8: JAG AMBUSH!

Az Zubayr, March 23

The tragic deaths of three un-embedded reporters caught in the crossfire between Fedayeen and tankers of the 1st Tank Battalion near the town of Az Zubayr led to a little known but intense firefight between Iraqi irregulars and the most unlikely of Marines- a team of legal and public affairs soldiers and their protection team. Tasked with investigating the shooting of the reporters by General Mattis, the staff judge advocate and divisional public affairs officer drove toward Az Zubayr in a convoy of two unarmed HMMWVs. As they entered the town, a black clad Fedayeen launched the first RPG toward the approaching vehicles…

SCENARIO INFORMATION

Duration of Game: 6 Turns

Initiative: US for duration of game

Special Conditions:

- Fedayeen are Irregulars – this is an Asymmetric Engagement.
- Air Defense Environment: Light Air Defense

Fog of War: Determined normally by Reaction Test rolls

Table Size: 2' x 3'

COMBAT AT KARBALA, 2004

HISTORICAL OUTCOME

The Iraqi militia was surprised by the arrival of two unarmed HMMWVs apparently unaware that the town still held Fedayeen defenders. Both HMMWVs were engaged by multiple RPGs and small arms fire as they raced through the town. The Marines returned effective fire but not before several were wounded. Turning around in Az Zubayr, the Marines managed to bypass hastily erected Fedayeen roadblocks and sped safely back to a nearby British VCP.

USMC MISSION

The small convoy of HMMWVs must extricate themselves from the ambush and escape back the way they came. Speed and suppressive fire will be the key to their success. The two HMMWVs begin the game on the main road into Az Zubayr.

USMC VICTORY POINTS

- Escape off-board with both HMMWVs operational at end of Turn 6: 10pts
- Exfiltrate all Marines, including wounded, off-board at end of Turn 6: 5pts
- No USMC KIA/POW at end of Turn 6: 3pts

A TYPICAL UNARMED HUMVEE TROOP CARRIER

USMC FORCE

USMC Basic Attributes

Initiative Level: D8

Confidence Level: Confident

Supply Level: Normal

Body Armor: Standard (1D)

Troop Quality/Morale: D8/D10

USMC Element

   Alpha One Zero

   (Mounted in lead unarmed HMMWV)

   1 x Marine Staff Officer w/9mm M9

   1 x Driver w/M16A2

   1 x Rifleman w/M16A2

   1 x Marine Staff Officer w/M16A2

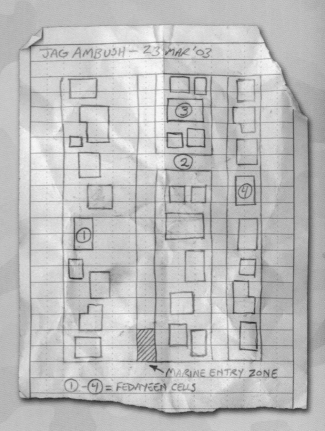

Alpha One One

(Mounted in trail unarmed HMMWV)

1 x Marine Officer w/Mossberg shotgun

1 x NCO w/M16A2

IRAQI MISSION

The local Fedayeen of Az Zubayr cannot believe the luck when look outs reported the two HMMWVs racing toward their town. Suspecting a trap and wary of American helicopter gunships, the Fedayeen stay concealed until the HMMWVs are about to enter the built up area before springing their ambush.

IRAQI VICTORY POINTS

- Destroy a HMMWV: 10pts
- Immobilize a HMMWV: 5pts
- Each Marine KIA/Serious WIA or captured Marine: 1pt

IRAQI FORCE

Iraqi Basic Attributes

Initiative Level: D6

Confidence Level: Confident

Supply Level: Normal

Body Armor: N/A

Troop Quality/Morale: D6/D12

Fedayeen

1 x Fedayeen Leader w/AK

Fedayeen Cell One

1 x Fedayeen leader w/AK

1 x Gunner w/RPG (Med. AP:2/AT:1(M))

3 x Irregulars w/AK

Fedayeen Cell Two

1 x Gunner w/RPG (Med. AP:2/AT:1(M))

5 x Irregulars w/AK

Fedayeen Cell Three

1 x Fedayeen leader w/AK

1 x Gunner w/RPG (Med. AP:2/AT:1(M))

1 x Gunner w/RPK (Lt. AP:1/AT:0)

3 x Irregulars w/AK

Fedayeen Cell Four

1 x Gunner w/RPG (Med. AP:2/AT:1(M))

5 x Irregulars w/AK

SPECIAL RULES

BUILDINGS

All buildings are rated at 6D8 and provide Solid Cover. They have not been reinforced.

OUT OF CONTACT MOVEMENT

The Fedayeen may use Out of Contact Movement.

CONTACT, WAIT OUT!

Instead of firing or driving, any one Marine in a HMMWV may attempt to raise British forces operating nearby. Due to the different communications nets in operation and the need for a message to be relayed, roll a TQ check to see if the contact report and request for assistance is successful. If so, two British WMIK Land Rovers and two Snatch Land Rovers from the British QRF will arrive on the main road, at the same entry point as the Marines, two turns later. They will engage any opposition forces in line of sight however will not enter the town until they can establish the location of the Marines. This is accomplished when a USMC leader figure uses his activation to "pop smoke" or launch a star-cluster – the figure may not add his Firepower to any attacks or perform any other actions during the activation it pops smoke.

If the Marines are in line of sight, the WMIKs will provide fire support while two infantry bricks dismount from the Snatches and advance to support the trapped Marines. The British are rated at TQ/Morale D8/D10. The WMIKs each mount a MAG58 GPMG and an M2 while the Snatches are unarmed.

Side-arms and Shotguns

Use the rules as detailed in the main rulebook. Shotguns throw an extra die in Close Combat (as do handguns) or within Optimum Range. Beyond Optimum, the FP of the shotgun is reduced to D6. Side-arms, like the 9mm M9, fire at a die shift down within Optimum Range (in this case D6) while are completely ineffective beyond Optimum Range.

US Navy SEALs, Persian Gulf, 2003

Anti-Tank RPG Warheads

Each time an RPG is fired, roll 1D6. If Iraqi regular forces, a roll of 4–6 indicates an AT RPG (Hvy. AP:3/AT:2(M). If Fedayeen or foreign jihadists, a 5–6 indicates an AT RPG.

SCENARIO 9: AL KUT

Al Kut, April 3

Marine General Mattis wanted to give the Iraqis the impression that the Marines were going to focus on the city of Al Kut and fight through the city toward Baghdad. In fact his plan called for RCT-1 to conduct a classic pincer movement on Al Kut and effectively fix Iraqi forces there while elements of RCT-5 and RCT-7 used the deception, and the shield created by RCT-1, to assault nearby An Nu'maniyah and seize the bridge across the Tigris which would give the Marines a straight run on the capital. If the Iraqi forces could be forced into the open by the ground assaults, amassed Coalition air power could destroy them. If they instead chose to fight to the death, Marine infantry and armor would eliminate them as a threat.

Scenario Information

Duration of Game: 8 Turns

Initiative: US begins game with Initiative, test on following turns.

Special Conditions:

- Fedayeen are Irregulars
- Air Defense Environment: Medium Air Defense

Fog of War: Determined normally by Reaction Test rolls

Table Size: 3' x 3'

USMC Mission

The USMC force is charged with assaulting and seizing the buildings surrounding the intersection so that Marine units can pass through and clear other parts of

HISTORICAL OUTCOME

The advance towards Baghdad was marked by few significant battles and none were larger than battalion size. In fact, small bloody firefights were more common with the Iraqis, not surprisingly, taking the lion's share of the damage. Although the Iraqi army was a shell of the one which had challenged the Coalition of Desert Storm, there was an element in Iraqi Freedom missing from Desert Storm that made it deadlier.

Coalition forces were now confronted by an often suicidal enemy. They would sell their lives cheaply in a series of hit and run skirmishes that sometimes built into pitched battles as Coalition forces sought to locate, close with and destroy them. Civilians were often used as shields and a disturbingly large number of civilian cars filled with explosives and driven by foreign fighters attracted by the promise of martyrdom were sent hurtling towards Coalition forces. The action portrayed in this scenario should serve to demonstrate the fanaticism of some of the opposition Coalition forces faced on the road to Baghdad. While training and proper application of firepower often overcame fanaticism, it still led to some hair-raising engagements.

the city. Once the intersection is secured, attempt to clear out any other strong-points identified in the area.

The USMC force deploys on up to a 24" frontage (12" in either direction from table corner) of the SW corner of the table. Infantry may begin the game mounted in their AAV transport or dismounted.

USMC VICTORY POINTS

- Clear the buildings overlooking the intersection of enemy forces and hold these at end of Turn 8: 3pts per building held
- Clear out all other enemy strong-points in the area: 3pts
- Keep Marine casualties (KIA/Seriously WIA) under 10%: 3pts

USMC FORCE

USMC Basic Attributes
Initiative Level: D8
Confidence Level: High

Supply Level: Normal
Body Armor: Standard (1D)
Troop Quality/Morale: D8/D10

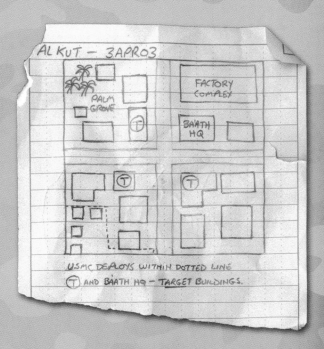

AL KUT — 3APR03

FACTORY COMPLEX

PALM GROVE

BAATH HQ

USMC DEPLOYS WITHIN DOTTED LINE
(T) AND BAATH HQ — TARGET BUILDINGS.

USMC Platoon

Platoon HQ

(Mounted in third AAV with Weapons Squad)

1 x Platoon Commander w/M16A2

1 x Platoon ('Gunny') Sergeant w/M16A2

1 x RTO w/M16A2

1 x ANGLICO FAC w/M16A2

USMC Rifle Squad One (mounted in first AAV)

1 x Squad Leader w/M16A2

Fire Team One Alpha

1 x Fire Team Leader w/M16A2

1 x Grenadier w/M203 (Lt. AP:1/AT:0)

1 x Gunner w/M249 (Lt. AP:1/AT:0)

1 x Rifleman w/M16A2

Fire Team One Bravo

1 x Fire Team Leader w/M16A2

1 x Grenadier w/M203 (Lt. AP:1/AT:0)

1 x Gunner w/M249 (Lt. AP:1/AT:0)

1 x Rifleman w/M16A2

US MARINES ASSAULTING PAST A USMC M1A1 INTO AL KUT. (PHOTO BY PIERS BRAND, FIGURES BY ELHEIM MINIATURES, M1 BY DRAGON MODELS)

Fire Team One Charlie

1 x Fire Team Leader w/M16A2

1 x Grenadier w/M203 (Lt. AP:1/AT:0)

1 x Gunner w/M249 (Lt. AP:1/AT:0)

1 x Rifleman w/M16A2

1 x AAVTP-7 Amtrac

USMC Rifle Squad Two (mounted in second AAV)

1 x Squad Leader w/M16A2

Fire Team Two Alpha

1 x Fire Team Leader w/M16A2

1 x Grenadier w/M203 (Lt. AP:1/AT:0)

1 x Gunner w/M249 (Lt. AP:1/AT:0)

1 x Rifleman w/M16A2

Fire Team Two Bravo

1 x Fire Team Leader w/M16A2

1 x Grenadier w/M203 (Lt. AP:1/AT:0)

1 x Gunner w/M249 (Lt. AP:1/AT:0)

1 x Rifleman w/M16A2

Fire Team Two Charlie

1 x Fire Team Leader w/M16A2

1 x Grenadier w/M203 (Lt. AP:1/AT:0)

1 x Gunner w/M249 (Lt. AP:1/AT:0)

1 x Rifleman w/M16A2

1 x AAVTP-7 Amtrac

Attached Weapons Squad (mounted in third AAV)

1 x Squad Leader w/M16A2

M240G GPMG Weapon Team

1 x Gunner w/M240G (Med. AP:2/AT:0)

2 x Riflemen w/M16A2

SMAW Team
1 x Gunner w/SMAW (Med. AP:4/AT:2(H) with +1 Positive Die shift to FP when attempting to destroy a building)
1 x Rifleman w/M16A2

Scout Sniper Team
1 x Sniper w/M40A3
1 x Spotter w/M16A2

1 x AAVTP-7 Amtrac

Attached Tank Section
2 x M1A1 Abrams

IRAQI MISSION

An Nu'maniyah and Al Kut are refuge to the remnants of the Republican Guard "Baghdad" Division which is positioned to cause harm to the Coalition's soft under belly, its supply lines. It appeared that the Marines planned to bypass the towns, but now word has been received that Marines are attacking into Al Kut. It appears that after the lessons of An Nasiriya the Coalition will not leave a major force intact behind its lines of advance. If Iraqi forces can hold out in these towns, the Coalition will be forced to divert forces to root them out. This could prove costly in men, equipment and most importantly, time.

The Iraqi force is charged with taking up a blocking position at a crossroads in Al Kut. Members of the Saddam Fedayeen have been assigned to "inspire" the force, which is battle weary and disheartened. The crossroad must be held at all costs! All Republican Guard infantry units must deploy in the buildings directly adjacent to the intersection. The heavy weapons, Fedayeen and armor can deploy anywhere on the board.

IRAQI VICTORY POINTS

- Hold the crossroads and deny it to the Marines by having forces still in at least one building at end of Turn 8: 10pts
- Hold any other building in the city in order to deny Marines a sector clear of enemy at end of Turn 8: 3pts
- KIA, Serious WIA or captured Marines: 1pt

IRAQI FORCE

Iraqi Basic Attributes
Initiative Level: D6
Confidence Level: Confident
Supply Level: Normal
Body Armor: N/A
Troop Quality/Morale: Varies. See below.

US NAVY SEAL, OPERATION IRAQI FREEDOM, 2003

A REPUBLICAN GUARD T-55 MBT. (PHOTO BY PIERS BRAND, FIGURE BY ELHEIM, VEHICLE BY BRITANNIA)

Iraqi Republican Guard (TQ/Morale D6/D8)

Platoon Command

1 x Iraqi Army RG Officer w/AK (TQ/Morale D6/D10)

1 x RTO w/AK

1 x NCO w/AK

Attached Armor

2 x T-55 MBTs

2 x BMP-1 APCs

SPG-9 73mm Recoilless Rifle Team

1 x Gunner w/SPG-9 Recoilless Rifle (Hvy. AP:3/AT:2(L)

2 x Crew w/AKs

Rifle Squad One

Fire Team One

6 x Riflemen w/AK

Fire Team Two

2 x Riflemen w/AK

1 x Gunner w/RPG (Med. AP:2/AT:1(M)

1 x Gunner w/RPK (Lt. AP:1/AT:0)

Rifle Squad Two

Fire Team One

6 x Riflemen w/AK

Fire Team Two

2 x Riflemen w/AK

1 x Gunner w/RPG (Med. AP:2/AT:1(M)

1 x Gunner w/RPK (Lt. AP:1/AT:0)

Rifle Squad 3

Fire Team One

6 x Riflemen w/AK

Fire Team Two

2 x Riflemen w/AK

1 x Gunner w/RPG (Med. AP:2/AT:1(M)

1 x Gunner w/RPK (Lt. AP:1/AT:0)

Fedayeen (TQ/Morale D6/D12)

1 x Fedayeen Leader w/AK

REPUBLICAN GUARDS MEET THE INVADERS ON THE OUTSKIRTS OF AL KUT. (PHOTO BY PIERS BRAND, FIGURES BY ELHEIM)

Fedayeen Cell One

1 x Fedayeen leader w/AK

1 x Gunner w/RPG (Med. AP:2/AT:1(M)

5 x Irregulars w/AK

Fedayeen Cell Two

1 x Fedayeen leader w/AK

1 x Gunner w/RPG (Med. AP:2/AT:1(M)

4 x Irregulars w/AK

Fedayeen Cell Three

1 x Fedayeen leader w/AK

1 x Gunner w/RPG (Med. AP:2/AT:1(M)

1 x Gunner w/RPK (Lt. AP:1/AT:0)

4 x Irregulars w/AK

Fedayeen RPG Team (no weapons team bonus)

1 x Gunner w/RPG with AT warheads (Hvy. AP:3/AT:2(M)

1 x Irregular w/AK

Suicide Vehicle Borne Improvised Explosive Device

(SVBIED – AP:8/AT:8(H), 8" radius)

2 x Soft skin cars or SUVs packed with explosives and driven by foreign volunteers.

SPECIAL RULES

BUILDINGS

All buildings are rated at 6D8 and provide Solid Cover. They have not been reinforced.

OUT OF CONTACT MOVEMENT

The Fedayeen may use Out of Contact Movement.

HUEY!

On Turn 4 onward, the attached Marine ANGLICO may attempt to call in an orbiting UH-1N Huey with

A US MARINE MANS THE .50 CALIBER MACHINE GUN ABOARD A USMC UH-1N "HUEY" HELICOPTER

mounted .50 door guns to provide close air support. Use standard TAC rules to resolve.

SCENARIO 10: THE FOOTBRIDGE

Diyala River, April 7

With many battles behind them, the Marines of RCT-7 faced one final obstacle at the gates to Baghdad: the Tigris River. Kilo Company of 3/7 was assigned to conduct an opposed assault across a small pedestrian bridge adjacent to a destroyed road bridge spanning the Diyala River, a tributary of the Tigris. The footbridge itself had also been damaged by artillery, leaving a large hole in the middle of the span. The Marines would have to close the gap prior to storming the far side. After crossing, the Marines of Kilo Company would have to spread out and hold the bridgehead to allow the rest of the 3rd battalion to pass. The Marine mission was one for which they had not traditionally trained– conducting an opposed bridge seizure in a major urban center. The action at the foot bridge would become one of those events that earn a place in Marine Corps history.

Historical Outcome

The Iraqi defense was not up to the task of holding the Diyala River line. Although the Marines of Kilo Company had to repair the bridge under fire and were funneled into what should have been a killing ground, they suffered minimal casualties. Several crew served weapons sited to target anyone crossing the bridge, including a heavy machine gun and recoilless rifle were discovered abandoned. The destruction of a Marine Amtrac by skillful artillery guidance from an Iraqi officer on a cell phone shows the price the Marines might have had to pay if the defense had been tougher.

Scenario Information

Duration of Game: 8 Turns
Initiative: US begins game with Initiative, test on following turns.
Special Conditions:
- Fedayeen are Irregulars
- Air Defense Environment: Medium Air Defense

Fog of War: Determined normally by Reaction Test rolls
Special Assets:
USMC: AH-1W Cobra Gunship
Iraqi Republican Guard: Light Artillery with Artillery Officer FO
Table Size: 2' x 3'

USMC Mission

The USMC must force a crossing of the footbridge spanning the Diyala River, clear the buildings opposite and establish a protective perimeter so reinforcements can cross.

USMC Victory Points

- Establish bridgehead with at least one fire team on the northern bank of the Diyala the end of Turn 8: 10pts
- Each civilian casualty caused by USMC fire: 1pt
- Keep Marine casualties (KIA or Serious WIA) to less than 10% of the committed force: 3pts

USMC Force

USMC Basic Attributes
Initiative Level: D8
Confidence Level: Confident
Supply Level: Normal
Body Armor: Standard (1D)
Troop Quality/Morale: D8/D10

USMC Platoon
   Platoon HQ
   (Mounted in third AAV with Weapons Squad)

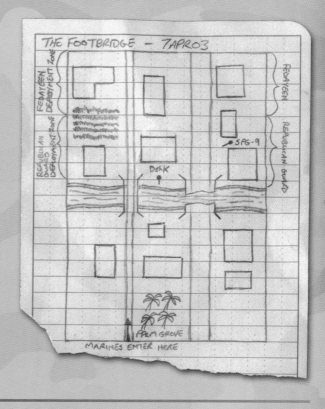

1 x Platoon Commander w/M16A2
1 x Platoon ('Gunny') Sergeant w/M16A2
1 x RTO w/M16A2
1 x ANGLICO FAC w/M16A2

USMC Rifle Squad One (mounted in first AAV)
1 x Squad Leader w/M16A2

Fire Team One Alpha
1 x Fire Team Leader w/M16A2
1 x Grenadier w/M203 (Lt. AP:1/AT:0)
1 x Gunner w/M249 (Lt. AP:1/AT:0)
1 x Rifleman w/M16A2

Fire Team One Bravo
1 x Fire Team Leader w/M16A2
1 x Grenadier w/M203 (Lt. AP:1/AT:0)
1 x Gunner w/M249 (Lt. AP:1/AT:0)
1 x Rifleman w/M16A2

Fire Team One Charlie
1 x Fire Team Leader w/M16A2
1 x Grenadier w/M203 (Lt. AP:1/AT:0)
1 x Gunner w/M249 (Lt. AP:1/AT:0)
1 x Rifleman w/M16A2

1 x AAVTP-7 Amtrac

USMC Rifle Squad Two (mounted in second AAV)
1 x Squad Leader w/M16A2

Fire Team Two Alpha
1 x Fire Team Leader w/M16A2
1 x Grenadier w/M203 (Lt. AP:1/AT:0)
1 x Gunner w/M249 (Lt. AP:1/AT:0)
1 x Rifleman w/M16A2

Fire Team Two Bravo
1 x Fire Team Leader w/M16A2
1 x Grenadier w/M203 (Lt. AP:1/AT:0)
1 x Gunner w/M249 (Lt. AP:1/AT:0)
1 x Rifleman w/M16A2

Fire Team Two Charlie
1 x Fire Team Leader w/M16A2
1 x Grenadier w/M203 (Lt. AP:1/AT:0)
1 x Gunner w/M249 (Lt. AP:1/AT:0)
1 x Rifleman w/M16A2

1 x AAVTP-7 Amtrac

Attached Weapons Squad (mounted in third AAV)
1 x Squad Leader w/M16A2

M240G GPMG Weapon Team
1 x Gunner w/M240G (Med. AP:2/AT:0)
2 x Riflemen w/M16A2

Javelin Team
1 x Gunner w/Javelin ATGM (AP:4/AT:4(H), Deck Attack)
1 x Rifleman w/M16A2

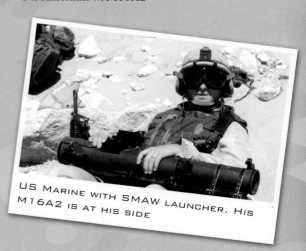

US MARINE WITH SMAW LAUNCHER. HIS M16A2 IS AT HIS SIDE

SMAW Team
1 x Gunner w/SMAW (Med. AP:4/AT:2(H) with +1 Positive Die shift to FP when attempting to destroy a building)
1 x Rifleman w/M16A2

Scout Sniper Team
1 x Sniper w/M40A3
1 x Spotter w/M16A2

1 x AAVTP-7 Amtrac

Iraqi Mission

The forward defenses of the city have been breached and the response to the call for a popular uprising against the Coalition forces has fallen below expectations. Our loyal forces have manned the defenses prepared in advance of this final encounter. The Republican Guard along with elements of the Saddam Fedayeen, the Ba'athist paramilitary forces, foreign Jihadists and the regular army has taken up the scimitar.

The enemy cannot prevail as long as the defensive line along the river holds. Fortunately, the enemy's options are limited to a dangerous bridging operation or crossing a narrow footbridge under fire. Artillery and mortars are pre-registered onto the approaches to both bridges. The Republican Guard has hidden armor which may be available to repel the assault when it comes. In addition, we have great confidence that citizens loyal to the country and to Holy Islam will strike, willing to trade their lives for the defeat of the infidel.

Prevent the Marines from gaining a foothold on the Baghdad side of the river. Fight the enemy on the banks of the river and slaughter them as they attempt to cross.

US Navy SEAL, Operation Iraqi Freedom, 2003

Iraqi Victory Points
- No Marines north of river at end of game: 10pts
- Each civilian casualty caused by Marine fires: 1pt
- Each Marine KIA/Serious WIA or captured Marine: 1pt

Iraqi Force
Iraqi Basic Attributes
Initiative Level: D6
Confidence Level: Confident
Supply Level: Normal
Body Armor: N/A
Troop Quality/Morale: Varies. See below:

Iraqi Republican Guard (TQ/Morale D6/D8)
    Attached Armor
    2 x T-72 MBTs (enter anywhere along northern table edge on Turn 3)

Platoon Command
1 x Iraqi Army RG Officer (Troop Quality/Morale
D6/D10) w/AK
1 x RTO w/AK
1 x NCO w/AK

Forward Observer
1 x Iraqi Army RG Officer Forward Observer
(Troop Quality/Morale D6/D10) w/AK

SPG-9 73mm Recoilless Rifle Team
1 x Gunner w/SPG-9 Recoilless Rifle (Hvy.
AP:3/AT:2(L)
2 x Crew w/AKs

SA-7 MANPADS Team (Targets aircraft only)
1 x Gunner w/SA-7 MANPADS (AA Weapon,
AT:4(H)
1 x Assistant w/AK

DShK HMG Team
1 x Gunner w/DShK HMG (Hvy. AP:3/AT:1(L)
2 x Crew w/AKs

Rifle Squad One
Fire Team One
6 x Riflemen w/AK

Fire Team Two
2 x Riflemen w/AK
1 x Gunner w/RPG (Med. AP:2/AT:1(M)
1 x Gunner w/RPK (Lt. AP:1/AT:0)

Rifle Squad Two
Fire Team One
6 x Riflemen w/AK

Fire Team Two
2 x Riflemen w/AK
1 x Gunner w/RPG (Med. AP:2/AT:1(M)
1 x Gunner w/RPK (Lt. AP:1/AT:0)

Rifle Squad 3
Fire Team One
6 x Riflemen w/AK

Fire Team Two
2 x Riflemen w/AK
1 x Gunner w/RPG (Med. AP:2/AT:1(M)
1 x Gunner w/RPK (Lt. AP:1/AT:0)

Fedayeen (TQ/Morale D6/D12)
1 x Fedayeen Leader w/AK

Fedayeen Cell One
1 x Fedayeen leader w/AK
1 x Gunner w/RPG (Med. AP:2/AT:1(M)
5 x Irregulars w/AK

Fedayeen Cell Two
1 x Fedayeen leader w/AK
1 x Gunner w/RPG (Med. AP:2/AT:1(M)
4 x Irregulars w/AK

Fedayeen Cell Three
1 x Fedayeen leader w/AK
1 x Gunner w/RPG (Med. AP:2/AT:1(M)
1 x Gunner w/RPK (Lt. AP:1/AT:0)
4 x Irregulars w/AK

Fedayeen RPG Team (no weapons team bonus)
1 x Gunner w/RPG with AT warheads (Hvy.
AP:3/AT:2(M)
1 x Irregular w/AK

SPECIAL RULES

ROAD WORK

One Marine fire team may "fix" the hole in the bridge by remaining stationary to it for one turn and using planks to drop over the gap. It may only react to fire directed at it that turn and cannot take offensive action.

CIVILIANS ON THE BATTLEFIELD

Place 3 civilian mobs in-between the two central buildings on the northern side of the bridge. They will move randomly as per the main rules. The Iraqi leaders may attempt to convert them into armed hostile mobs per the rules, but only if Marines fire on any building with weapons heavier than 7.62mm small arms (M203/Mk19 40mm and heavier).

BUILDINGS

All buildings are rated at 6D8 and provide Solid Cover. They have not been reinforced.

OUT OF CONTACT MOVEMENT

The Fedayeen may use Out of Contact Movement.

THE SO-CALLED "EMPTY BATTLEFIELD" ISN'T AS EMPTY AS ONE MIGHT THINK. CIVILIANS WERE A CONSTANT CONCERN FOR COALITION FORCES

MARINE COUNTER BATTERY

The Marines have access to off-table counter battery radar and supporting artillery. On the turn immediately following an off board Iraqi indirect fire mission, the Marine player may roll a TQ opposed test against the TQ of his Iraqi counterpart with a successful roll indicating that counter battery fire has neutralized the Iraqi fire support for the remainder of a game.

IRAQI LIGHT ARTILLERY

The Iraqi FO can call on fire support from a battery of off-board light artillery. Use standard artillery rules including Danger Close.

COBRAS!

From the first turn onward, the Marine commander and/or his ANGLICO, may attempt to call in an orbiting AH-1W "Whisky" Cobra to provide close air support. Use standard TAC rules to resolve.

SCOWL FOR THE CAMERA!

An al Jazeera camera man is recording the action. Place with a random Iraqi unit. Any KIAs, WIAs or prisoners taken with the camera man in LOS adds an extra VP. If he is killed by USMC fire, the Marines take a -3 to their VPs to account for the negative media coverage. Roll a TQ check when the unit he is attached to is engaged with a failure indicating he has been hit.

ANTI-TANK RPG WARHEADS

Each time an RPG is fired, roll 1D6. If Iraqi regular forces, a roll of 4–6 indicates an AT RPG (Hvy. AP:3/AT:2(M)). If Fedayeen or foreign jihadists, a 5–6 indicates an AT RPG.

THE ARMORED SPEARHEAD: WITH THE US ARMY IN IRAQ

SCENARIO 11: THE HORNET'S NEST

Objective *Pistol*, Outside As Samawah, March 22

On March 22, 2003, a Hunter Killer Team (HKT) from C3-7 Cav "Crazy Horse" approached a canal bridge at Objective *Pistol*. Based on reports from an SOF unit in the area, the team expected to be greeted by Iraqi regulars eager to surrender. Instead, they became embroiled in a fierce firefight with irregular Saddam Fedayeen troops. This would be the Cav's first encounter with fanatical irregular troops in civilian garb, but it would be far from their last.

SCENARIO INFORMATION

Duration of Game: 8 Turns

Initiative: US for duration of game

Special Conditions:
- Fedayeen and Ba'athist Police are Irregulars – this is an Asymmetric Engagement.
- Air Defense Environment: Light Air Defense

Fog of War: Generated normally by Reaction Tests

Special Assets:

    US Force: Counter Battery (Off Board)

    Iraqi Force: Medium Mortars (Off Board)

Table Size: 3' x 4'
- **A:** Position of SSgt. Johnson's Bradley Fighting Vehicle
- **B:** Starting position of M1 Abrams Tank
- **1:** Truck pursued by SSgt. Johnson (Fedayeen Unit 1)
- **2–4:** Fedayeen Units
- **H:** Reinforcement Entry Point

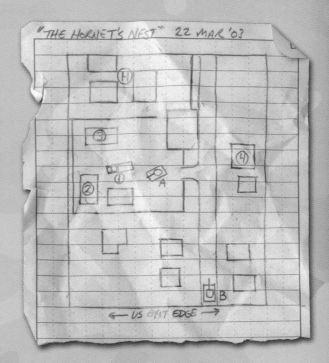

US ARMY MISSION

Staff Sergeant Johnson pursued a truck full of armed combatants into the courtyard of a large building complex with the intent of destroying the vehicle and its occupants. Unbeknownst to SSgt. Johnson, the complex housed a Fedayeen barracks and Ba'athist police headquarters. Johnson's Bradley weathered multiple waves of assault before he and the Abrams MBT accompanying him withdrew to await reinforcements to finish the job they'd started. They left hundreds of enemy dead behind.

US ARMY VICTORY POINTS
- Bradley remains within courtyard for 4 turns: 10pts

HISTORICAL OUTCOME

SSgt. Dillard Johnson's HKT team pursued a fleeing Iraqi army truck into a Fedayeen barracks and Ba'athist police compound. A point blank battle unfolded which pitted his Bradley IFVs and Abrams tank against hundreds of Fedayeen armed with small arms and RPGs. This battle introduced the US Army to the enemy's practice of utilizing taxis and ambulances as military personnel carriers and using civilian residences as fighting positions. It also erased any illusions that the mass surrenders that characterized the First Gulf War would apply to the new conflict.

SSgt. Dillard was wounded repeatedly in the engagement but continued to fight until its end.

- Bradley and M1 withdraw from table via marked exit point on map: 5pts.

US ARMY FORCE

US Army Basic Attributes

Initiative Level: D8
Confidence Level: Confident
Supply Level: Normal
Body Armor: Standard (1D)
Troop Quality/Morale: D8/D10

Element of Crazy Horse Hunter Killer Team
- 1 x Bradley Infantry Fighting Vehicle (with 2 x Dismounts w/M4s)
- 1 x M1A1 MBT

IRAQI FORCE MISSION

US armored vehicles are assaulting us in our own headquarters! Make the invaders pay!

IRAQI VICTORY POINTS

- Per Enemy Soldier Seriously Wounded/KIA: 3pts
- Per Enemy Soldier POW: 5pts
- Bradley IFV Immobilized or Destroyed: 5pts
- Abrams MBT Immobilized or Destroyed: 10pts

IRAQI FORCE

Iraqi Basic Attributes

Initiative Level: N/A
Confidence Level: Confident
Supply Level: Normal
Body Armor: N/A
Troop Quality/Morale: D6/D12

Fedayeen

Fedayeen Unit 1
(Loaded in truck at beginning of Turn 1)
1 x Fedayeen leader w/AK
1 x Gunner w/RPG (Med. AP:2/AT:1(M))
1 x Gunner w/RPK (Lt. AP:1/AT:0)
2D6 Riflemen w/AK

Fedayeen Unit 2
1 x Fedayeen leader w/AK
1 x Gunners w/RPG (Med. AP:2/AT:1(M))
1 x Gunner w/RPK (Lt.AP:1/AT:0)
3 x Riflemen w/AK

Fedayeen Unit 3
1 x Fedayeen leader w/AK
2 x Gunners w/RPG (Med. AP:2/AT:1(M))
5 x Riflemen w/AK

Fedayeen Unit 4
1 x Fedayeen leader w/AK
2 x Gunners w/RPG (Med. AP:2/AT:1(M))
5 x Riflemen w/AK

Reinforcements

All other Iraqi forces take the form of reinforcements that arrive at the beginning of each turn after the first. Roll 2D6 on the Reinforcement Table to determine who arrives. All reinforcements appear at the point marked "H" on the map

REINFORCEMENT TABLE

DIE ROLL	INSURGENT UNIT
2	1D6 w/Small Arms + 1 w/Lt. Support
3	1 w/Med. Support
4	1D6 w/Small Arms & ROLL AGAIN
5	1 w/Med. Support
6	1D6+2 w/Small Arms
7	1D6 w/Small Arms + Leader +1 Lt. Support
8	1D6+2 w/Small Arms
9	1D6 w/Small Arms + ROLL AGAIN
10	1w/Med. Support
11	1D6 w/Small Arms + Leader + Med. Support
12	2D6 w/Small Arms

Medium Support – Roll 1D6 for type:
1: AT RPG (Hvy. AP:3/AT:2(M)
2-4: RPG (Med. AP:2/AT:1(M)
5-6: PKM MG (Med. AP:2/AT:0)
For groups without leaders, roll 1D6. A roll of 1 adds 1 leader to the group.

SPECIAL RULES
RPG DUDS

The RPGs used in this engagement were apparently old and/or poorly manufactured. Dozens of duds bounced harmlessly off the Bradley. To represent this, apply a -1 die roll modifier to RPG Firepower dice rolls (i.e, a roll of 4 would be treated as a 3).

BUILDINGS

All buildings are rated at 6D8 and provide Solid Cover. They have not been reinforced.

SCENARIO 12: THAT AIN'T NO HILL FOR A STEPPER

The Najaf Escarpement, March 23

On 23 March, 1st BCT passed through 2nd BCT at Objective *Rams* and began its run on Objective *Raiders*. To reach *Raiders*, 1st BCT had to first assault over the Najaf Escarpment, a steep, 250 foot tall natural shelf running east and west between *Rams* and *Raiders*. The narrow road leading to the top of the escarpment had a nearly 12% grade in places. Waiting at the top of the escarpment were a major munitions storage area, emplaced anti-aircraft positions, and a Fedayeen Saddam training facility. Iraqi artillery and infantry fighting positions were dug into the escarpment's ridge to sweep its approaches, particularly the road. The equivalent of two battalions of Iraqi regulars and Fedayeen troops stood ready to block any thrust over the escarpment towards Baghdad.

Breaching this natural fortress fell to TF 3-69 AR. Supported by artillery, air, and a 1000 meter smoke-screen, TF 3-69 reached the top of the escarpment under a steady barrage of mortar and artillery fire. At the top of the escarpment, US forces split up to neutralize various enemy threats. US forces poured through the breach en route to other objectives, often fighting their way through impromptu enemy ambushes.

Once again, the Iraqis proved they were willing to stand and fight.

US NAVY SEAL, OPERATION IRAQI FREEDOM, 2003

HISTORICAL OUTCOME

In the end, the Escarpment fell without the loss of American life thanks to the efficient application of combined arms and daring close air support. With Najaf isolated and the escarpment more or less secured, the Army's road to Baghdad was open.

SCENARIO INFORMATION

Duration of Game: 8 Turns or less
Initiative: US for duration of game
Special Conditions:
- Fedayeen and Ba'athist Police are Irregulars – this is an Asymmetric Engagement.
- Air Defense Environment: Light Air Defense

Fog of War: Generated normally by Reaction Tests
Table Size: 2' x 2'
- C1–C5: Fedayeen Cells
- 1–5: Hot spots

US ARMY MISSION

A US Army HEMTT hauling fuel has become bogged down in deep sand in the middle of an ongoing ambush at the top of the escarpment. The vehicle's crew has abandoned it and it is only a matter of time before the Fedayeen Saddam get lucky and blow it to kingdom come. Every ounce of fuel is vital to the success of the invasion, so a cool headed senior NCO quickly gathers an ad hoc assault team to drive off the Fedayeen and, more importantly, drive the HEMTT to safety!

US ARMY VICTORY POINTS

- Each Insurgent casualty: 1pt
- No friendlies captured by insurgents: 5pts
- HEMTT driven off table: Victory!

US ARMY FORCE

US Army Basic Attributes
Initiative Level: D8

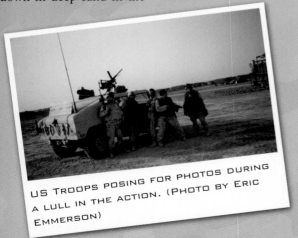

US TROOPS POSING FOR PHOTOS DURING A LULL IN THE ACTION. (PHOTO BY ERIC EMMERSON)

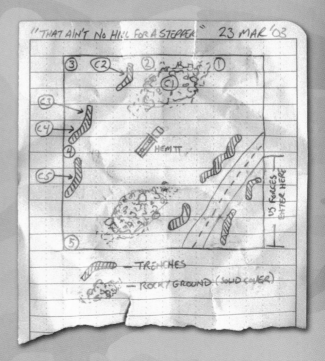

Confidence Level: Confident
Supply Level: Normal
Body Armor: Standard (1D)
Troop Quality/Morale: D8/D10

Team 1
1 x Platoon Sgt. w/M4
1 x Grenadier w/M203 (Lt. AP:1/AT:0)
4 x Riflemen w/M4

Team 2
1 x Team Leader w/M4
2 x Gunners w/M249 (Lt. AP:1/AT:0)
2 x Riflemen w/M4

Team 3
1 x Team Leader w/M4
1 x Gunner w/M249 (Lt. AP:1/AT:0)
1 x Gunner w/M203 (Lt. AP:1/AT:0)
2 x Riflemen w/M4

IRAQI FORCE MISSION

Destroy the American invaders! Destroy the fuel truck and leave their tanks gasping for fuel!

IRAQI VICTORY POINTS

- Per enemy soldier wounded: 1pt
- Per enemy soldier KIA: 2pts
- Per enemy soldier POW: 3
- HEMTT destroyed: Victory!

IRAQI FORCE

Iraqi Basic Attributes
Initiative Level: N/A (Irregulars)
Confidence Level: Normal
Supply Level: Normal

Body Armor: N/A
Troop Quality/Morale: D6/D10

Fedayeen

Fedayeen Cell 1
1 x Leader w/AK
1 x Gunner w/RPK (Lt. AP:1/AT:0)
1 x Gunner w/RPG (Med. AP:2/AT:1(M)
2 x Insurgents w/AKs

Fedayeen Cell 2
1 x Leader w/AK
1 x Gunner w/RPG (Med. AP:2/AT:1(M)
4 x Insurgents w/AKs

Fedayeen Cell 3
1 x Leader w/AK
6 x Insurgents w/AKs

Fedayeen Cell 4
1 x Leader w/AK
1 x PKM MG (Med.)
1 x Insurgent w/AKs

Fedayeen Cell 5
1 x Leader w/AK
1 x Gunner w/RPK (Lt. AP:1/AT:0)
1 x Gunner w/RPG (Med. AP:2/AT:1(M)
2 x Insurgents w/AKs

Reinforcements

At the end of each turn, roll 2D6 on the Reinforcement table to determine what reinforcements arrive for the insurgents. Roll to see which Hot Spot they arrive from. If a roll on the table results in the arrival of multiple units, roll Hot Spots for each unit.

AN HEMTT ON A RAPID REFUELING OPERATION IN IRAQ, 2003

THE HEMTT

The Heavy Expanded Mobility Tactical Truck (HEMTT) is a sturdy, eight-wheeled truck used to haul fuel, supplies, and even other vehicles. The HMTT was designed to keep up with rapid moving M1 tank companies, a task at which it proved successful. While a soft-skin, the HMTT is large and durable – as a result, it can take a decent amount of pounding and "keep on trucking."

Use the following vehicle description for the HEMTT in this scenario:

If the HEMTT is brewed up or immobilized, it is considered "destroyed" for the purposes of Insurgent Victory conditions.

To drive the HEMTT off the table, a US unit must spend a complete turn with the vehicle. At least two of the unit's members must be actively starting and unsticking

REINFORCEMENT TABLE

DIE ROLL	INSURGENT UNIT
2	1D6 w/Small Arms + 1 w/Lt Support.
3	1 w/Med. Support
4	1D6 w/Small Arms & ROLL AGAIN
5	1 w/Med. Support
6	1D6+2 w/Small Arms
7	1D6 w/Small Arms + Leader +1 Lt. Support
8	1D6+2 w/Small Arms
9	1D6 w/Small Arms + ROLL AGAIN
10	1 w/Medium Support
11	1D6 w/Small Arms + Leader + Med. Support
12	2D6 w/Small Arms

Medium Support – Roll 1D6 for type:
1: AT RPG (Hvy. AP:3/AT:2(M)
2-4: RPG (Med. AP:2/AT:1(M)
5-6: PKM MG (Med. AP:2/AT:0)
For groups without leaders, roll 1D6. A roll of 1 adds 1 leader to the group.

SPECIAL RULES

END GAME

The game ends when the HEMTT is driven off the table or destroyed or at the end of Turn 8, whichever comes first.

US SPECIAL FORCES, IRAQ, 2003

NAME	CLASS	TYPE	FIREPOWER	GUN RATING	MGs	FRONT ARMOR	SIDE ARMOR	REAR ARMOR	DECK ARMOR	CREW	ATTRIBUTES/ NOTES
HEMTT	S	W	Unarmed	N/A	N/A	3D6	3D6	3D6	1D6	2+4	Very Large

the big vehicle, so reduce the unit's Firepower accordingly. At the beginning of the next turn, the unit may drive the HEMTT (the unit may be Split if desired). In the soft sand, the HEMTT can only move at Tactical speed.

ANTI-TANK RPG WARHEADS

Each time an RPG is fired, roll 1D6. If Iraqi regular forces, a roll of 4–6 indicates an AT RPG (Hvy. AP:3/AT:2(M). If Fedayeen or foreign jihadists, a 5–6 indicates an AT RPG.

SCENARIO 15: MEDAL OF HONOR

Near the Baghdad International Airport, April 4

Lead elements of the US 3rd Infantry Division have taken Baghdad International Airport, and have established blocking positions on the main highway linking it with the Iraqi capital. 2nd Platoon, B Company, 11th Engineers have been tasked with creating a holding area for the large number of detainees expected in the next few days. A suitable location has been found, and preparations are under way when a large enemy force is spotted attempting to outflank the American position. Calling for reinforcements, the Engineers prepare to make a stand.

SCENARIO INFORMATION

Duration of Game: See **Special Rules**

Initiative: US Army for duration of game

Special Conditions:

- Iraqi forces are Irregulars – this is an Asymmetric Engagement.
- Air Defense Environment: Light Air Defense

Fog of War: Generated normally by Reaction Tests

Table Size: 2' x 2'

- I1–I5: Insurgent Cells
- A, B: US Fireteams
- CE: Casualty Evacuation point
- 1–5: Hot spots

US ARMY MISSION

The US force must make the area secure by eliminating all insurgents from the area. US casualties must be kept to a minimum.

US ARMY VICTORY POINTS

- Each Insurgent casualty: 1pt
- No friendlies captured by insurgents: 5pts

US ARMY FORCE

US Army Basic Attributes

Initiative Level: D8

Confidence Level: Confident

Supply Level: Normal

Body Armor: Standard (1D)

Troop Quality/Morale: D8/D8 unless otherwise noted

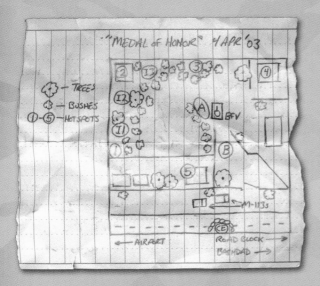

HISTORICAL OUTCOME

This scenario is based on the actions of SFC Paul R. Smith and 2nd Platoon, Bravo Company, 11th Engineer Battalion, 3rd Infantry Division.

On April 4, 2003, a 100-man force was assigned to block the highway between Baghdad and the airport, about one mile east of the airport. A brief battle was fought, and several Iraqi prisoners were captured. SFC Smith spotted a walled enclosure nearby with a tower overlooking it. He and his squad set about building an impromptu enemy prisoner of war (EPW) holding area for prisoners in the enclosure. Smith and sixteen other men used an Armored Combat Earthmover (similar to a bulldozer) to knock a hole in the south wall of the courtyard. On the north side, there was a metal gate that Smith assigned several men to guard. These men noticed fifty to 100 Iraqi troops who had taken positions in trenches just past the gate.

Smith summoned a Bradley fighting vehicle to attack their position. Three nearby M113 Armored Personnel Carriers came to support the attack. An M113 was hit, possibly by a mortar, and all three crewmen were injured.

The Bradley, running low on ammunition and damaged, withdrew during a lull in the battle. Smith organized the evacuation of the injured M113 crewmen. However, behind the courtyard was a military aid station crowded with 100 combat casualties. To protect it from being overrun, Smith chose to fight on rather than withdraw with the wounded.

Meanwhile, some Iraqis had taken position in the tower overlooking the courtyard, just over the west wall. The Iraqis now had the Americans in the courtyard under an intense crossfire. Smith took command of the M113 and ordered a driver to position it so that he could attack both the tower and the trenches. He manned the M113's machine gun, going through three boxes of ammunition. A separate team, led by First Sergeant Tim Campbell attacked the tower from the rear, killing the Iraqis.

As the battle ended, Smith's machine gun fell silent. His comrades found him slumped in the turret hatch. His armored vest was peppered with thirteen bullet holes, the vest's ceramic armor inserts, both front and back, cracked in numerous places. But the fatal shot, one of the last from the tower, had entered his neck and passed through the brain, killing SFC Smith.

For his actions during the battle, Sergeant First Class Smith was posthumously awarded the Medal of Honor.

The US player has the following forces, which should be deployed as indicated on the map.

Position A (Deployed in a skirmish line facing west)

1 x Platoon Sergeant w/M4 (TQ/Morale: D8/D12, +2 to Morale Rolls)

1 x Squad Leader w/M4 and AT4 (Hvy. AP:3/AT:3(H)) (TQ/Morale: D8/D12)

Fireteam One

1 x Fireteam leader w/M16A2

1 x Gunner w/M249 (Lt. AP:1/AT:0)

1 x Grenadier w/M203 (Lt. AP:1/AT:0)

Fireteam Two (w/Concertina Wire)

1 x Fireteam leader w/M16A2

1 x Gunner w/M249 (Lt. AP:1/AT:0)

1 x Grenadier w/M203 (Lt. AP:1/AT:0)

Casualty Evacuation Point:

1 x Company First Sergeant w/M4 (TQ/Morale: D10/D10)

1 x Medic w/M16A2

Vehicles

1 x M2A2 BFV

3 x Crew, no dismounts. *Vehicle is critically low on ammo. Any time a 1 is rolled on attack dice reduce the firepower of all the tank's weapons by one die. When the number is reduced to a single die, the vehicle must attempt to withdraw (by exiting the SE corner of the board) to replenish ammunition. Likewise, if the vehicle*

suffers any type of vehicle breakdown due to enemy action, it will attempt to withdraw as above.

2 x M113A2 APC

3 x Crew each, no dismounts. Each vehicle is also carrying 2 x AT4 (Hvy. AP:3/AT:3(H)) that may be issued as required.

Reinforcements

2x Fire Teams, each:

2 x Riflemen w/M16A2

1 x Gunner w/M249 (Lt. AP:1/AT:0)

1 x Gunner w/M203 (Lt. AP:1/AT:0)

The first team is available the turn after the U.S. player suffers his first casualty. The second team is available the turn after any Insurgent forces are spotted south of the highway retaining wall. All reinforcements may enter anywhere along the south board edge.

IRAQI FORCE MISSION

Overrun the enemy roadblock from behind. Cause as much damage and inflict as many casualties as possible!

IRAQI VICTORY POINTS

- Per Regular wounded: 1pt
- Per Regular KIA: 2pts
- Per Vehicle Damaged: 2pts
- Per Vehicle Destroyed: 5pts
- Per Captive held at end of game: 5pts
- Per Insurgent that exits south east corner: 5pts

IRAQI FORCE

Iraqi Basic Attributes

Initiative Level: N/A (Irregulars)

Confidence Level: Confident

Supply Level: Normal

Body Armor: N/A

Troop Quality/Morale: D6/D10

The Insurgent forces begin deployed in prepared positions (+1 Defense Die) as indicated on the map. Each Insurgent group (A, B & C) consists of the following: 1 x Leader and 9 x Insurgents (1 w/RPG, 1 w/MG, 1 x 60mm Mortar, 6x AK).

All other insurgent forces are randomly determined reinforcements.

Reinforcements

The Insurgency Level of the game is 4. At the end of each turn, the Insurgent player will roll 1D6. On a roll 4 or less, new Insurgent fighters will arrive from a random Hot Spot. Roll to see which Hot Spot they arrive from. If a roll on the table results in the arrival of multiple units, roll Hot Spots for each unit.

To determine what "reinforcements" arrive, roll 2D6 on the following table:

DIE ROLL	INSURGENT UNIT
2	1D6 w/Small Arms + 1 w/Lt. Support
3	1 w/Med. Support
4	1D6 w/Small Arms & ROLL AGAIN
5	1 w/Med. Support
6	1D6+2 w/Small Arms
7	1D6 w/Small Arms + Leader +1 Lt. Support
8	1D6+2 w/Small Arms
9	1D6 w/Small Arms +ROLL AGAIN
10	1w/Med. Support
11	1D6 w/Small Arms +Leader +Med. Support
12	2D6 w/Small Arms

Medium Support – Roll 1D6 for type:
1: AT RPG (Hvy. AP:3/AT:2(M)
2-4: RPG (Med. AP:2/AT:1(M)
5-6: PKM MG (Med. AP:2/AT:0)
For groups without leaders, roll 1D6. A roll of 1 adds 1 leader to the group.

SPECIAL RULES

END GAME

The game ends when there are no (non-casualty) Regular forces remaining, or Insurgent casualty total (including those who quit the field) exceeds 100.

CONCERTINA WIRE

Concertina wire takes 1 activation to cross. Units crossing concertina wire may perform no other action while doing so. Units firing at them receive a +1 Troop Quality die shift. Concertina wire may be deployed or recovered in one action by Engineers with proper equipment (gloves, etc.).

MAXIMUM INSURGENT FORCE SIZE

At no time will the Insurgent player have more than 50 figures on the board at a time. Number and types of support weapons are limited by the figures available.

NEUTRALIZING HOT SPOTS

Hot Spots can only be neutralized (temporarily) by physically occupying them; they may not be permanently eliminated.

BUILDINGS

All buildings apart from the marked casualty evacuation point are rated at 6D8 and provide Solid Cover. They have not been reinforced. The CEP has been fortified with dirt, sand bags, etc., for a building strength of 6D10.

ANTI-TANK RPG WARHEADS

Each time an RPG is fired, roll 1D6. If Iraqi regular forces, a roll of 4–6 indicates an AT RPG (Hvy. AP:3/AT:2(M)). If Fedayeen or foreign jihadists, a 5–6 indicates an AT RPG.

SCENARIO 14: THUNDER RUN ON HIGHWAY 8

Highway 8, April 5

The OIF concept of operations called for the Marines and Army to envelope the capital, establishing a multi-layered cordon before airborne and airmobile units would assault the city in sectors. While attempting to avoid the much feared Stalingrad scenario of block by bloody block street fighting in Baghdad, the Army's Task Force 1-64 of the 2nd 'Spartan' Brigade of the 3rd Infantry Division was tasked with what was officially an armored reconnaissance into Baghdad to test the defenses. Unofficially it was known as the Thunder Run. On April 5, the men of Task Force 1-64, the 'Desert Rogues' advanced north onto Highway 8 and headed for Baghdad…

HISTORICAL OUTCOME

The first Thunder Run by 3ID lasted for some three hours before the armored convoy eventually linked up with Task Force 2-7 Infantry holding Baghdad International Airport (BIAP). The Desert Rogues met stiff but poorly organized resistance from a mixture of Republican Guard, Iraqi Regular Army, Saddam Fedayeen and foreign jihadists including a number of suspected suicide car bombers. Task Force 1-64 arrived at BIAP with one dead, several wounded and missing one M1A1 which had suffered a mobility kill. Every vehicle however was pock-marked with small arms, RPG and recoilless rifle strikes. Iraqi losses were, perhaps not surprisingly, much heavier with something in the region of 800 to 2000 KIA, one T-72, one BMP-1, thirty odd trucks and numerous ZPU anti-aircraft platforms destroyed.

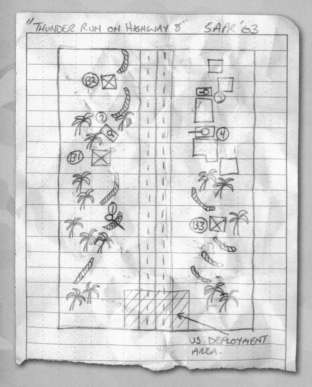

SCENARIO INFORMATION

Duration of Game: 8 Turns

Initiative: US Army for duration of game

Special Conditions:

- Fedayeen are Irregulars
- Air Defense Environment: Light Air Defense

Fog of War: Generated normally by Reaction Tests

Table Size: 4' x 6'

- B1–B3: Bunkers
- 1: SPG-9 Revetment
- 2, 3: BMP
- 4: T-55 MBT

US Army Mission

The objective of the Task Force 1-64 element is to advance across the board, suppressing or destroying Iraqi defenses and exit the northern end of the table while minimizing friendly and civilian casualties.

US Army Victory Points

- Exit with all vehicles operational from the Northern table edge at end of Turn 8: 10pts
- No friendly casualties (Serious WIA, KIA or captures): 5pts
- No civilian casualties at end of Turn 6: 3pts

US Army Force

US Army Basic Attributes

Initiative Level: D8

Confidence Level: High

Supply Level: Normal

Body Armor: Standard (1D)

Troop Quality/Morale: D8/D10

Task Force 1-64 Lead Element

2 x M1A1 (deploy unbuttoned)

2 x M2A2 ODS (deploy unbuttoned)

Each carrying 6 dismounted infantry scouts:

1 x Fire Team Leader w/M4

2 x Grenadier w/M203 (Lt. AP:1/AT:0)

1 x Gunner w/M249 (Lt. AP:1/AT:0)

2 x Riflemen w/M4

TYPICAL ROADSIDE BUNKERS ERECTED BY THE FEDAYEEN

1 x M113A3 with ACAV kit mounting M2 .50 (Hvy. AP:4/AT:1(L), deploy unbuttoned)

Carrying an engineer fire team:

1 x Fire Team Leader w/M16A2

1 x Grenadier w/M203 (Lt. AP:1/AT:0)

1 x Gunner w/M249 (Lt. AP:1/AT:0)

1 x Rifleman w/M16A2

1 x M113A3 Band Aid mounting M2 .50 (Hvy. AP:4/AT:1(L), deploy unbuttoned)

Carrying a field medical team:

1 x Medic w/M16A2

2 x Combat Life Savers w/M16A2

2 x Riflemen w/M16A2

Iraqi Mission

Contrary to everything proclaimed by the Iraqi leadership, the Americans have broken through your lines and are driving into the capital! You must defend Baghdad! A mixture of Republican Guard and Saddam Fedayeen are racing to man bunkers and trenches along Highway 8. Stop or at least slow the advance of the Americans to allow promised reinforcements to arrive and repulse the invaders.

Iraqi Victory Points

- Destroy a vehicle: 10pts
- Immobilize a vehicle: 5pts
- Each Marine KIA/Serious WIA or captured Marine: 1pt

Iraqi Force

Iraqi Basic Attributes

Initiative Level: D6

Confidence Level: Normal

Supply Level: Normal

Body Armor: N/A

Troop Quality/Morale: Varies. See below.

Iraqi forces can be set up anywhere on the table other than the US deployment zone. They may be deployed hidden at the beginning of the game.

Iraqi Republican Guard (TQ/Morale D6/D8)

Attached Armor

1 x T-55 MBT

2 x BMP-1

Platoon Command

1 x Iraqi Army RG Officer w/AK (TQ/Morale: D6/D10)

1 x RTO w/AK

1 x NCO w/AK

Forward Observer

1 x Iraqi Army RG Officer Forward Observer w/AK (TQ/Morale D6/D10)

SPG-9 73mm Recoilless Rifle Team

1 x Gunner w/SPG-9 Recoilless Rifle (Hvy. AP:3/AT:2(L)

2 x Crew w/AKs

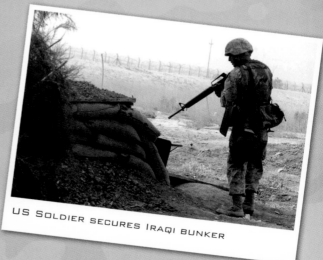

US Soldier secures Iraqi bunker

DShK HMG Team One
1 x Gunner w/DShK HMG (Hvy. AP:3/AT:1(L)
2 x Crew w/AKs

DShK HMG Team Two
1 x Gunner w/DShK HMG (Hvy. AP:3/AT:1(L)
2 x Crew w/AKs

Rifle Squad One
Fire Team One
6 x Riflemen w/AK

Fire Team Two
2 x Riflemen w/AK
1 x Gunner w/RPG (Med. AP:2/AT:1(M)
1 x Gunner w/RPK (Lt. AP:1/AT:0)

Rifle Squad Two
Fire Team One
6 x Riflemen w/AK

Fire Team Two
2 x Riflemen w/AK
1 x Gunner w/RPG
(Med. AP:2/AT:1(M)
1 x Gunner w/RPK (Lt.
AP:1/AT:0)

Rifle Squad Three
Fire Team One
6 x Riflemen w/AK

Fire Team Two
2 x Riflemen w/AK
1 x Gunner w/RPG (Med. AP:2/AT:1(M)
1 x Gunner w/RPK (Lt. AP:1/AT:0)

Rifle Squad Four
Fire Team One
6 x Riflemen w/AK

Fire Team Two
2 x Riflemen w/AK
1 x Gunner w/RPG (Med. AP:2/AT:1(M)
1 x Gunner w/RPK (Lt. AP:1/AT:0)

Fedayeen (Irregulars, TQ/Morale D6/D12)
Fedayeen Cell One
1 x Fedayeen leader w/AK
1 x Gunner w/RPG (Med. AP:2/AT:1(M)
4 x Irregulars w/AK

Fedayeen Cell Two
1 x Fedayeen leader w/AK
2 x Gunners w/RPG (Med. AP:2/AT:1(M)
4 x Irregulars w/AK

Fedayeen Cell Three
1 x Fedayeen leader w/AK
1 x Gunner w/RPG (Med. AP:2/AT:1(M)
1 x Gunner w/RPK (Lt. AP:1/AT:0)

Fedayeen RPG Team One (no weapons team bonus)
1 x Fedayeen leader w/AK
1 x Gunner w/RPG with AT warheads (Hvy. AP:3/AT:2(M)
1 x Irregular w/AK

Fedayeen RPG Team Two (no weapons team bonus)
1 x Fedayeen leader w/AK
1 x Gunner w/RPG with AT warheads (Hvy. AP:3/AT:2(M))
1 x Irregular w/AK

SPECIAL RULES

OUT OF CONTACT MOVEMENT

The Fedayeen may use Out of Contact Movement.

ARMY COUNTER BATTERY

3ID have access to off-table counter battery radar and supporting artillery. On the turn immediately following an off board Iraqi indirect fire mission, the US player may roll a TQ opposed test against the TQ of his Iraqi counterpart with a successful roll indicating that counter battery fire has neutralized the Iraqi fire support for the remainder of a game.

IRAQI LIGHT ARTILLERY

The Iraqi FO can call on fire support from a battery of off-board light artillery. Use standard artillery rules including Danger Close.

CONFUSED MOTORISTS OR VBIEDs?

CIVILIANS ON THE BATTLEFIELD

At the beginning of the game, players must place three civilian mobs on the table, with each player placing a mob in turn. The Iraqi player will place the first and last mob on the table. Iraqi leaders may attempt to convert these mobs into armed mobs.

CIVILIAN OR CAR BOMBER?

Each turn roll 1D6. On a 5–6, a civilian vehicle has driven onto the board- on a 5 from the south, on a 6 from the north. US elements can fire warning shots at the vehicles as their action once they are within optimum range of small arms or at any range with non-explosive vehicle mounted weapons (coax, .50 or loader's M240). Instead of carrying out a normal attack, roll an opposed TQ check against the Iraqi player.

If successful, the vehicle turns around immediately and drives off-board. If not successful, the vehicle continues toward US forces. Once within range to ram the first US vehicle, the Iraqi player rolls a 1D6. On a 1-3, the civilian vehicle continues safely past the US element. On a 4-5, the vehicle contains Ba'athist fanatics and they ram the closest vehicle or group of infantry dismounts with a 4D6 attack. On a 6, it is a Suicide Vehicle Borne Improvised Explosive Device (SVBIED) (FP 8D6, 8" radius) packed with explosives and driven by foreign volunteers which will detonate using the standard car bomb rules.

TRENCHES, BUNKERS, BUILDINGS AND PALM GROVES

The Iraqi trenches count as Improved Cover (+2d); the bunkers as Fortified Cover (+3d); the buildings are rated 6D8; and the palm groves provide a Solid Cover (+1d) cover bonus as long as fighters are within 2" of a palm.

ANTI-TANK RPG WARHEADS

Each time an RPG is fired, roll 1D6. If Iraqi regular forces, a roll of 4–6 indicates an AT RPG (Hvy. AP:3/AT:2(M)). If Fedayeen or foreign jihadists, a 5–6 indicates an AT RPG.

OPTIONAL RULES

AMBIENT FIRE

As per the Ambient Fire rules against helicopters, you may introduce Ambient Fire against each US ground call sign to simulate the relentless fire encountered on Highway 8. Each turn, the Iraqi player may roll a 3D8 attack against each vehicle and dismounted infantry element on the board- this simulates both small arms and RPG fire- in addition to all normal firing. This can prove to be quite lethal and is only recommended once you have played the basic scenario at least once.

SCENARIO 45: COJONE EH

Highway 8, April 5

During the lightning Thunder Run of April 5, the men of Task Force 1-64, were engaged by hundreds of enemy fighters along Highway 8. While virtually every vehicle was hit by small arms fire and many were struck by RPGs, none were immobilized by a so-called 'mobility kill' apart from one M1A1 Abrams, call-sign Charlie One Two but better known from its barrel art, 'Cojone Eh'. Charlie One Two was hit by an unlucky recoilless rifle or RPG round into the rear engine housing which caused a fuel fire on the rear deck. The tank's crew bravely tried to fight the blaze to save the vehicle while taking increasingly heavy fire from Iraqis in trench-lines, shipping containers and bunkers on both sides of the highway.

SCENARIO INFORMATION

Duration of Game: 6 Turns

HISTORICAL OUTCOME

After a heroic effort to stem the fire and fighting back close quarter Fedayeen attacks, often with their side-arms and M4s, the crew of Charlie One Two finally abandoned their track and cross-decked to other vehicles in the convoy. The TC of Charlie One Two cut the fuel lines and opened the blast doors on the ammunition storage before dropping in thermite grenades. The trail tank added a shot from its 120mm main gun for good measure to deny the stricken vehicle to the enemy. In a testament to the awesome survivability of the Abrams, the vehicle survived the fire and a Maverick ATGM launched by the USAF in an air strike and was later used in propaganda videos by the Iraqis.

Initiative: US Army for duration of game

Special Conditions:

- Fedayeen are Irregulars – this is an Asymmetric Engagement.
- Air Defense Environment: Light Air Defense

Fog of War: Generated normally by Reaction Tests

Table Size: 4' x 6'

- 1: ACAV
- 2: Charlie One Two (immobilized M1A1)
- 3: Charlie Six Six (M1A1)
- 4: M2A2 BFV
- B1–B3: Bunkers 1 through 3
- T1, T2: Trenches 1 and 2

US ARMY MISSION

The objective of the Task Force 1-64 element is two-fold; deny the enemy the propaganda value of a recovered Abrams and ensure the crew and other vehicles in the element safely exit the board.

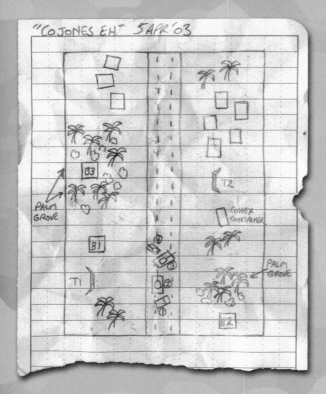

US Army Victory Points

- Deny Charlie One Two by recovering all sensitive materials and deploying thermite grenades by end of Turn 6: 5pts
- Exit with all vehicles operational, apart from Charlie One Two, from the Northern table edge at end of Turn 6: 5pts
- No friendly casualties (Serious WIA, KIA or captures): 5pts

US Army Force

US Army Basic Attributes

Initiative Level: D8

Confidence Level: High

Supply Level: Normal

Body Armor: Standard (1D)

Troop Quality/Morale: D8/D10

Task Force 1-64 Element

Charlie One Two

1 x M1A1 (immobilized but TC and loader MGs still operable) Carrying:

1 x TC w/M4

1 x Gunner w/M4

1 x Loader w/M4

1 x Driver w/M4

Charlie Six Six

1 x M1A1 (deploy unbuttoned, has hydraulic issues and cannot traverse turret)

1 x M2A2 ODS (deploy unbuttoned)

Carrying 6 dismounted infantry scouts:

1 x Fire Team Leader w/M4

2 x Grenadier w/M203 (Lt. AP:1/AT:0)

1 x Gunner w/M249 (Lt. AP:1/AT:0)

2 x Riflemen w/M4

1 x M113A3 with ACAV kit mounting M2 .50 (Hvy. AP:4/AT:1(L), deploy unbuttoned)

Carrying the First Sergeant and his fire team:

1 x First Sergeant with M16A2

1 x Fire Team Leader w/M16A2

1 x Grenadier w/M203 (Lt. AP:1/AT:0)

1 x Gunner w/M249 (Lt. AP:1/AT:0)

1 x Rifleman w/M16A2

Iraqi Force Mission

Your brave Fedayeen have disabled one of the mighty American tanks! Press home the victory by killing the crew, immobilizing other vehicles and capturing the disabled tank.

Iraqi Victory Points

- Destroy a vehicle: 10pts
- Immobilize a vehicle: 5pts
- KIA/Serious WIA or captured crew of Charlie One Two: 5pts
- Each Marine KIA/Serious WIA or captured Marine: 1pt

Iraqi Force

Iraqi Basic Attributes

Initiative Level: D6
Confidence Level: Confident
Supply Level: Normal
Body Armor: N/A
Troop Quality/Morale: TQ/Morale D6/D12

Fedayeen

Fedayeen Cell One (deploy in Conex Container)
1 x Fedayeen leader w/AK
1 x Gunner w/RPG (Med. AP:2/AT:1(M)
3 x Irregulars w/AK

Fedayeen Cell Two (deploy in Bunker One)
1 x Fedayeen leader w/AK
2 x Gunners w/RPG (Med. AP:2/AT:1(M)
3 x Irregulars w/AK

Fedayeen Cell Three (deploy in Bunker Two)
1 x Fedayeen leader w/AK
1 x Gunner w/RPG (Med. AP:2/AT:1(M)
1 x Gunner w/PKM (Med. AP:2/AT:0)

Fedayeen Cell Four (deploy in Bunker Three)
1 x Fedayeen leader w/AK
1 x Gunner w/RPG (Med. AP:2/AT:1(M)
1 x Gunner w/PKM (Med. AP:2/AT:0)

Fedayeen Cell Five (deploy in Trench One)
1 x Fedayeen leader w/AK
1 x Gunner w/RPG (Med. AP:2/AT:1(M)
5 x Irregulars w/AK

Fedayeen Cell Six (deploy in Trench Two)
1 x Fedayeen leader w/AK
1 x Gunner w/RPG (Med. AP:2/AT:1(M)
4 x Irregulars w/AK

Fedayeen RPG Team One
(no weapons team bonus, deploy in palm grove)
1 x Fedayeen leader w/AK
2 x Gunners w/RPG with AT warheads (Hvy. AP:3/AT:2(M))

Reinforcements

On Turn 2 and every turn thereafter, reinforcements automatically arrive for the Saddam Fedayeen as the Iraqis flock to the disabled tank, and may be placed up to 6" from any board edge.

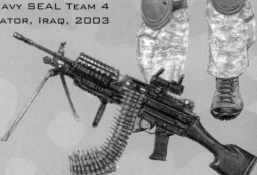

US Navy SEAL Team 4 Operator, Iraq, 2003

REINFORCEMENT TABLE

ROLL 1D10:
(ALL STATS TQ/MORALE D6/D10)

Roll	Reinforcement
1.	3 x Irregulars w/AK, 1 x Leader w/AK
2.	4 x Irregulars w/AK, 1 x Leader w/AK, 1 x Gunner w/Med. Support
3.	1 x Gunner w/Med. Support, 1 x Irregular w/AK
4.	1 x SVD Dragunov sniper, 1 x Irregular w/AK
5.	1 x Gunner w/PKM (Med. AP:2/AT:0), 1 x Irregular w/AK
6.	1 x 60mm light mortar with 1 x crew and 1 x spotter with AK
7.	6 x Irregulars w/AK, 1 x Leader w/AK, 1 x Gunner w/Med. Support
8.	5 x Irregulars w/AK, 1 x Leader w/AK, 1 x Gunner w/Med. Support, 1 x RPK gunner
9.	1 x DShK HMG (Hvy. AP:3/AT:1(L) with 3 x crew w/AKs
10.	1 x SPG-9 Recoilless Rifle (Hvy. AP:3/AT:2(L) with 3 x crew w/AKs

Medium Support – Roll 1D6 for type:
1:     AT RPG (Hvy. AP:3/AT:2(M)
2-4:   RPG (Med. AP:2/AT:1(M)
5-6:   PKM MG (Med. AP:2/AT:0)

SPECIAL RULES

ABANDON TANK!

The crew of Charlie One Two must spend the first two turns of the game attempting to extinguish the fire, sanitize the vehicle and prep it for demolition by thermite grenades. During this time they must stay on or within 1" of the tank and can only react in Rounds of Fire with their M4 carbines. At the start of Turn 3 they are considered to have completed their tasks and dropped thermite grenades into the turret and can act normally.

TANK OR TAXI?

The crew can evacuate by riding on the still operable Charlie Six Six or by mounting up in the M113- there is no room available in the Bradley. If the crew of Charlie

One Two rides out on the deck of Charlie Six Six, it cannot fire either its main gun or coax, leaving only the TC and Loader turret MGs to fire (with non-buttoned up crew rules to apply).

CHARLIE SIX SIX

While the crew and the dismounts are on the ground Charlie Six Six cannot engage targets with its main gun due to the close proximity of infantry and the risk from the concussion effects of the 120mm. Additionally it has recurring problems with its hydraulics and cannot turn its turret and must turn the whole vehicle to engage targets with its coax.

OUT OF CONTACT MOVEMENT

The Fedayeen may use Out of Contact Movement.

CIVILIAN OR CAR BOMBER?

Each turn roll 1D6. On a 5–6, a civilian vehicle has driven onto the board- on a 5 from the south, on a 6 from the north. US elements can fire warning shots at the vehicles as their action once they are within optimum range of small arms or at any range with non explosive vehicle mounted weapons (coax, .50 or loader's M240). Instead of carrying out a normal attack, roll an opposed TQ check against the Iraqi player.

If successful, the vehicle turns around immediately and drives off-board. If not successful, the vehicle continues toward US forces. Once within range to ram the first US vehicle, the Iraqi player rolls a 1D6. On a 1–3, the civilian vehicle continues safely past the US element. On a 4–5, the vehicle contains Ba'athist fanatics and they ram the closest vehicle or group of infantry dismounts with a 4D6 attack. On a 6, it is a Suicide Vehicle Borne Improvised Explosive Device (SVBIED) (FP 8D6, 8" radius) packed with explosives and driven by foreign volunteers which will detonate using the standard car bomb rules.

TRENCHES, BUNKERS, BUILDINGS AND PALM GROVES

The Iraqi trenches count as Improved Cover (+2d); the bunkers and Conex as Fortified Cover (+3d); the buildings 6D8; and the palm groves provide a Solid Cover (+1d) cover bonus as long as fighters are within 2" of a palm.

ANTI-TANK RPG WARHEADS

Each time an RPG is fired, roll 1D6. If Iraqi regular forces, a roll of 4–6 indicates an AT RPG (Hvy. AP:3/AT:2(M)). If Fedayeen or foreign jihadists, a 5–6 indicates an AT RPG.

OPTIONAL RULES

AMBIENT FIRE

As per the Ambient Fire rules against helicopters, you may introduce Ambient Fire against each US ground call sign to simulate the relentless fire encountered on Highway 8. Each turn, the Iraqi player may roll a 3D8 attack against each vehicle and dismounted infantry element on the board- this simulates both small arms and RPG fire- in addition to all normal firing. This can prove to be quite lethal and is only recommended once you have played the basic scenario at least once.

SCENARIO 46: THE DEFENSE OF OBJECTIVE CURLY

Baghdad, April 7

The second Thunder Run into the capital occurred on April 7th. Three key East West highway intersections along Highway 8 into the center of Baghdad were identified as vital to hold and defend to safeguard the already over-stretched supply line to the advancing armor. These were named Objectives *Larry*, *Moe* and *Curly*. Objective *Curly* was considered the least likely to be heavily defended and was assigned to an ad-hoc task force of some eighty Army personnel from the Third Battalion, 15th Infantry under Captain Harry Hornbuckle. His force consisted of a single mechanised infantry platoon and five M2A2 Bradleys, four M1114 HMMWVs, four M1064A3s mounting 120mm mortars, three M557s, four M113s carrying engineers, two M9 ACE bulldozers, an M88 recovery vehicle and an M113 Band Aid tracks along with some attached Special Forces in pickup trucks. As they rolled into the objective to secure it, Hornbuckle's men spotted trenches dug under the highway overpasses and realised that perhaps *Curly* may be a harder fight than they had imagined...

HISTORICAL OUTCOME

Objective *Curly* consisted of a cloverleaf intersection with ramps running up and down the highway. Surrounding the intersection was a collection of two and three story apartments, an administration building, a factory and a multi-story hotel. All were occupied by a mixture of Saddam Fedayeen and foreign jihadists. Additionally, Iraqi irregulars had taken up a mixture of positions both under the ramps and overpasses and on top of them, enabling them to fire down on the Americans. The firefight at *Curly* lasted some seven hours and proved to be the most vicious battle of all three objectives. TF 1-15 suffered suicide car bombs, drive bys by armed technicals, human wave assaults and even friendly fire from supporting artillery. They were finally reinforced and held the intersection, allowing the vital supplies to continue to flow to the units at the tip of the spear.

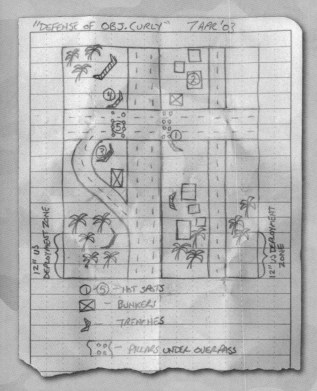

Scenario Information

Duration of Game: 6 Turns

Initiative: US for duration of game

Special Conditions:

- Fedayeen are Irregulars – this is an Asymmetric Engagement.
- Air Defense Environment: Medium Air Defense

Fog of War: Generated normally by Reaction Tests

Table Size: 4' x 5'

US Army Mission

The objective of the Hornbuckle's Task Force 3-15 is to hold the intersection for 8 turns while minimizing friendly casualties.

US Army Victory Points

- Hold the intersection at the end of Turn 8 (no enemy units within 6" of the underpass): 10pts

- No friendly casualties (Serious WIA, KIA or captures): 5pts

US Army Force

US Army Basic Attributes

Initiative Level: D8

Confidence Level: High

Supply Level: Normal (lowers to Poor after Turn 6 to simulate the tremendous amount of fire)

Body Armor: Standard (1D)

Troop Quality/Morale: D8/D10 except for Special Forces who are D10/D10

Task Force 3-15 Element

   3 x M2A2 ODS (deploy unbuttoned)

   Each carrying 6 dismounted infantry scouts:

   1 x Fire Team Leader w/M4

   2 x Grenadier w/M203 (Lt. AP:1/AT:0)

   1 x Gunner w/M249 (Lt. AP:1/AT:0)

   2 x Riflemen w/M4

1 x M113A3 with ACAV kit mounting M2 .50 (Hvy. AP:4/AT:1(L) – deploy unbuttoned) Carrying the Company Sergeant Major and his fire team:

1 x CSM with M16A2

1 x Fire Team Leader w/M16A2

1 x Grenadier w/M203 (Lt. AP:1/AT:0)

1 x Gunner w/M249 (Lt. AP:1/AT:0)

1 x Rifleman w/M16A2

1 x M1064A3 with ACAV kit mounting M2 .50 (Hvy. AP:4/AT:1(L) – deploy unbuttoned) Carrying a 120mm mortar team:

1 x Fire Team Leader w/M16A2

1 x Mortar Man w/M203 (Lt. AP:1/AT:0)

3 x Mortar Man w/M16A2

2 x M1114 Up-armored HMMWVs

Each carrying a Scout fire team:

1 x Fire Team Leader w/M4

1 x Grenadier w/M203 (Lt. AP:1/AT:0)

1 x Gunner w/M249 (Lt. AP:1/AT:0)

1 x Rifleman w/M4

1 x M113A3 Band Aid mounting M2 .50 (Hvy.
AP:4/AT:1(L) – deploy unbuttoned) Carrying a
field medical team:

1 x Medic w/M16A2

2 x Combat Life Savers w/M16A2

2 x Riflemen w/M16A2

1 x Toyota Pick Up mounting M240G (Med.
AP:3/AT:0)

Carrying a four man Special Forces team;

1 x SF Captain w/Mk11

2 x SF NCO w/M4/M203 (Lt. AP:1/AT:0)

1 x SF NCO w/M249 (Lt. AP:1/AT:0)

IRAQI FORCE MISSION

Press home the attack on the Americans and ensure the
precious fuel for their tanks cannot get through. This is
the final line of defense before the infidels enter Baghdad
– make them pay for their folly.

VICTORY POINTS

- Destroy a vehicle: 10pts
- Immobilize a vehicle: 5pts
- Each Marine KIA/Serious WIA or captured: 2pts

IRAQI FORCE

Iraqi Basic Attributes

Initiative Level: D6

Confidence Level: Normal

Supply Level: Normal

Body Armor: N/A

Troop Quality/Morale: TQ/Morale D6/D12

Fedayeen and Foreign Fighters

Cell One (deploy in Trench at Hot Spot One)

1 x Leader w/AK

1 x Gunner w/RPG (Med. AP:2/AT:1(M)

5 x Irregulars w/AK

Cell Two (deploy in Trench at Hot Spot Two)

1 x Leader w/AK

2 x Gunners w/RPG (Med. AP:2/AT:1(M)

1 x Gunner w/RPD (Lt. AP:1/AT:0)

4 x Irregulars w/AK

Cell Three (deploy in Trench at Hot Spot Three)

1 x Leader w/AK

1 x Gunner w/RPG (Med. AP:2/AT:1(M)

1 x Gunner w/PKM (Med. AP:2/AT:0)

2 x Irregulars w/AK

Cell Four (deploy in Bunker at Hot Spot Four)

1 x Leader w/AK

1 x Gunner w/RPG (Med. AP:2/AT:1(M)

1 x Gunner w/PKM (Med. AP:2/AT:0)

1 x Irregular w/AK

Cell Five (deploy on Overpass at Hot Spot Five)

1 x Leader w/AK

1 x Gunner w/RPG (Med. AP:2/AT:1(M)

6 x Irregulars w/AK

RPG Team One (no weapons team bonus, deploy
anywhere within 6" of a Hot Spot)

1 x Leader w/AK

2 x Gunners w/RPG with AT warheads
(Hvy. AP:3/AT:2(M)

Saddam Fedayeen on the move with a typical "technical." (Photo by Piers Brand, figures by Elheim, vehicle by S&S Models)

RPG Team Two (no weapons team bonus, deploy anywhere within 6" of a Hot Spot)
2 x Gunners w/RPG with AT warheads (Hvy. AP:3/AT:2(M))
2 x Irregulars w/AK

SPG-9 Team (no weapons team bonus, deploy anywhere within 6" of a Hot Spot)
1 x Leader w/AK
1 x Gunner w/SPG-9 RR (Hvy. AP:3/AT:2(L))
2 x Crew w/AK

Fedayeen Technicals
1 x Technical mounting a 12.7mm DShK (Hvy. AP:4/AT:1(L)) and crewed by driver, passenger, gunner and assistant gunner (all with personal AKs)
1 x Technical mounting a 7.62mm PKM (Med. AP:3/AT:0) and crewed by driver, passenger, gunner and assistant gunner (all with personal AKs)

2 x Suicide Vehicle Borne Improvised Explosive Device (SVBIED) (FP 8D6, 8" radius)
Soft skin cars or SUVs packed with explosives and driven by foreign volunteers. These must deploy on board anywhere on highway or the parallel road within 6" of any board edge.

Reinforcements
On Turn 2 and every turn thereafter, reinforcements automatically arrive for the Fedayeen and the foreign fighters and are placed using the Hot Spot rules.

REINFORCEMENT TABLE
Roll 1D10:
(ALL STATS TQ/Morale D6/D12)

1.	5 x Irregulars w/AK, 1 x Leader w/AK
2.	6 x Irregulars w/AK, 1 x Leader w/AK, 1 x Gunner w/Med. Support
3.	2 x Gunner w/Med. Support, 1 x Irregular w/AK
4.	1 x SVD Dragunov sniper
5.	1 x Gunner w/PKM (Med. AP:2/AT:0), 1 x Irregular w/AK
6.	1 x 60mm light mortar with 1 x crew and 1 x spotter with AK
7.	4 x Irregulars w/AK, 1 x Leader w/AK, 1 x Gunner w/Med. Support
8.	5 x Irregulars w/AK, 1 x Leader w/AK, 1 x Gunner w/Med. Support, 1 x RPK gunner
9.	1 x DShK HMG (Hvy. AP:3/AT:1(L) with 3 x crew w/AKs
10.	1 x SPG-9 Recoilless Rifle (Heavy Support, AP:3/AT:2(L) with 3 x crew w/AKs

Medium Support – Roll 1D6 for type:
1: AT RPG (Hvy. AP:3/AT:2(M))
2-4: RPG (Med. AP:2/AT:1(M))
5-6: PKM MG (Med. AP:2/AT:0)

SPECIAL RULES

OUT OF CONTACT MOVEMENT

The Fedayeen may use Out of Contact Movement.

CIVILIAN OR CAR BOMBER?

Each turn roll 1D6. On a 5–6, a civilian vehicle has driven onto the board – on a 5 from the south, on a 6 from the north. US elements can fire warning shots at the vehicles as their action once they are within optimum range of small arms or at any range with non-explosive vehicle mounted weapons (coax, .50 or loader's M240). Instead of carrying out a normal attack, roll an opposed TQ check against the Iraqi player.

If successful, the vehicle turns around immediately and drives off-board. If not successful, the vehicle continues toward US forces. Once within range to ram the first US vehicle, the Iraqi player rolls a 1D6. On a 1–3, the civilian vehicle continues safely past the US element. On a 4-5, the vehicle contains Ba'athist fanatics and they ram the closest vehicle or group of infantry dismounts with a 4D6 attack. On a 6, it is a Suicide Vehicle Borne Improvised Explosive Device (SVBIED) (FP 8D6, 8" radius) packed with explosives and driven by foreign volunteers which will detonate using the standard car bomb rules.

TRENCHES, BUNKERS, BUILDINGS AND PALM GROVES

The Iraqi trenches count as Improved Cover (+2d); the bunkers as Fortified Cover (+3d); the buildings as 6D8; and the palm groves provide a Solid Cover (+1d) cover bonus as long as fighters are within 2" of a palm.

A TYPICAL IRAQI PALM GROVE

AMBIENT FIRE

As per the Ambient Fire rules against helicopters, you may introduce Ambient Fire against each US ground call sign to simulate the huge amounts of RPG and small arms fire from the buildings surrounding the intersection. Each turn, the Iraqi player may roll a 3D8 attack against each vehicle and dismounted infantry element on the board- this simulates both small arms and RPG fire- in addition to all normal firing.

ANTI-TANK RPG WARHEADS

Each time an RPG is fired, roll 1D6. If Iraqi regular forces, a roll of 4–6 indicates an AT RPG (Hvy. AP:3/AT:2(M). If Fedayeen or foreign jihadists, a 5–6 indicates an AT RPG.

THE QUIET MEN: SPECIAL OPERATIONS ENGAGEMENTS

SCENARIO 17: SPRINT

While Marine and Army conventional forces advanced on Baghdad, a secret war was being fought by Coalition Special Operations Forces. In the South, Army ODAs and SEALs supported these conventional forces in reconnaissance, 'ground truth' intelligence gathering and agent handling and direct action operations. In the North, the ODAs with their Kurdish Peshmerga allies became the main effort after Turkey's refusal to allow the 4th Infantry Division's passage into Iraq. In the North and South West, British and Australian Special Air Service squadrons seized key sites and airfields, carried out reconnaissance missions and interdicted fleeing Iraqi leadership figures and foreign fighters flocking across the border. In the West, US Army Special Forces and the special operators of Task Force 20 conducted raids, psychological warfare and long range surveillance and reconnaissance operations. It was during one of these SR missions, along Highway 10 outside of the town of Ar Rutba that the men of US Army ODA 525 found themselves almost overrun by a fanatical Iraqi force…

SCENARIO INFORMATION

Duration of Game: 8 Turns
Initiative: ODA for duration of game
Special Conditions:
- Fedayeen are Irregulars – this is an Asymmetric Engagement.
- Air Defense Environment: Light Air Defense

Fog of War: Generated normally by Reaction Tests
Table Size: 4' x 4'

HISTORICAL OUTCOME

Deployed in a covert observation post, two operators from ODA 525 found themselves cut off from their colleagues by five Fedayeen technicals, tracing the tire tracks of the team's GMVs. The remainder of the ODA deployed a hasty ambush and used their GMV mounted crew served weapons to engage the technicals and force them to withdraw. Soon, the Iraqis returned, in far greater numbers. Over one hundred Fedayeen and several technical mounted DShKs began hunting for the ODA. As they closed in, the ODA transmitted the brevity code word 'Sprint' warning all nearby Coalition air assets that a Special Forces ground call sign was in danger of being overrun. Controlled by an orbiting AWACS, the responding fast air was soon stacked four high with the OP team calling in danger close air strikes on the encircling Iraqis. Other ODAs operating in the AO sped quickly toward the battle to assist. After a contact lasting some seven hours, the Iraqis finally withdrew back into Ar Rutba and the men of ODA 525 successfully exfiltrated with zero friendly casualties.

ODA MISSION

ODA 525 must safely exfiltrate the two-man OP while attempting to force back the advancing Iraqi forces and stop them from overrunning either the OP or the main ODA position.

ODA VICTORY POINTS

- Exfiltrate the OP team safely (no Serious Wounds) to the main ODA position by the end of Turn 8: 10pts

ODA FORCE

ODA Basic Attributes

Initiative Level: D8

Confidence Level: High

Supply Level: Abundant

Body Armor: Standard (1D)

Troop Quality/Morale: D10/D10

ODA OP (both are classed as SF JTAC/TAC)

   1 x SF NCO w/M4A1/M203 (Lt. AP:1/AT:0)

   1 x SF NCO w/Mk11

ODA 525 (begin game mounted in GMVs)

GMV One Alpha

GMV mounting 2 x M240G (Med. AP:3/AT:0) and

1 x Mk19 (Med. 2D/AT:0)

1 x SF Captain w/M4A1

1 x SF NCO w/Mk11

1 x SF NCO w/M4A1/M203 (Lt. AP:1/AT:0)

1 x SF NCO w/Minimi Para (Lt. AP:1/AT:0)

GMV One Bravo

GMV mounting 2 x M240G (Med. AP:3/AT:0) and

1 x M2HB (Hvy. AP:3/AT:1(L)

1 x SF Chief Warrant Officer w/M4A1

1 x SF NCO w/Mk11

1 x SF NCO w/M4A1/M203 (Lt. AP:1/AT:0)

1 x SF NCO w/Minimi Para (Lt. AP:1/AT:0)

GMV One Charlie

GMV mounting 2 x M240G (Med. AP:3/AT:0) and

1 x M2HB (Hvy. AP:3/AT:1(L)

1 x SF NCO w/M4A1

1 x SF NCO w/M82A1

SPECIAL FORCES OPERATORS WITH A TYPICAL GMV

IRAQI FORCE MISSION

American Special Forces have been conducting operations in your AO. They have a spotter on a hill outside of the town and are calling in murderous air strikes that are killing your men. They must be stopped before the air strikes demoralize your militia and allow the Americans to capture Ar Rutba.

IRAQI VICTORY POINTS

- KIA or Seriously Wound both members of the OP before the end of Turn 8: 10pts
- Each SF operator KIA/Serious WIA or captured: 2pts
- Each destroyed GMV: 5pts
- Each immobilized GMV: 2pts

IRAQI FORCE

Iraqi Basic Attributes

Initiative Level: D6

Confidence Level: Confident

Supply Level: Normal

Body Armor: N/A

Troop Quality/Morale: TQ/Morale D6/D10 (the Fedayeen have already been demoralized by the airstrikes and have suffered a dice down shift from their normal D12)

Initial Fedayeen Force

Fedayeen Cell One

1 x Fedayeen leader w/AK

1 x Gunner w/RPG (Med. AP:2/AT:1(M)

6 x Irregulars w/AK

Fedayeen Cell Two

1 x Fedayeen leader w/AK

2 x Gunners w/RPG (Med. AP:2/AT:1(M)

5 x Irregulars w/AK

Fedayeen Cell Three

1 x Fedayeen leader w/AK

2 x Gunners w/RPG (Med. AP:2/AT:1(M)

1 x Gunner w/RPK (Lt. AP:1/AT:0)

6 x Irregulars w/AK

Fedayeen Cell Four

1 x Fedayeen leader w/AK

1 x Gunner w/RPG (Med. AP:2/AT:1(M)

6 x Irregulars w/AK

Fedayeen Cell Five

1 x Fedayeen leader w/AK

1 x Gunner w/PKM (Med. AP:2/AT:0)

5 x Irregulars w/AK

Fedayeen RPG Team (no weapons team bonus)

1 x Fedayeen leader w/AK

1 x Gunner w/RPG with AT warheads (Hvy. AP:3/AT:2(M)

1 x Irregular w/AK

Fedayeen Technicals

2 x Technicals mounting a 12.7mm DShK (Hvy. AP:4/AT:1(L) and crewed by driver, passenger, gunner and assistant gunner (all with personal AKs)

2 x Technicals mounting a 7.62mm PKM (Med. AP:3/AT:0) and crewed by driver, passenger, gunner and assistant gunner (all with personal AKs)

Reinforcements

On Turn 2 and every turn thereafter, reinforcements automatically arrive for the Saddam Fedayeen and may be placed up to 6" from the eastern board edge.

REINFORCEMENT TABLE

Roll 1D10:
(all stats TQ/Morale D6/D10)

1.	4 x Irregulars w/AK, 1 x Leader w/AK
2.	4 x Irregulars w/AK, 1 x Leader w/AK, 1 x Gunner w/Med. Support
3.	1 x Gunner w/Med. Support, 1 x Irregular w/AK
4.	1 x SVD Dragunov sniper, 1x Irregular w/AK
5.	1 x Gunner w/PKM (Med. AP:2/AT:0), 1 x Irregular w/AK
6.	1 x 60mm light mortar with 1 x crew and 1 x spotter with AK
7.	6 x Irregulars w/AK, 1 x Leader w/AK, 1 x Gunner w/Med. Support
8.	6 x Irregulars w/AK, 1 x Leader w/AK, 1 x Gunner w/Med. Support, 1 x RPK gunner
9.	1 x Technical mounting DShK (AP:4/AT:1(L))
10.	Off Table 82mm Medium Mortar Barrage

Medium Support – Roll 1D6 for type:
1:     AT RPG (Hvy. AP:3/AT:2(M))
2-4:   RPG (Med. AP:2/AT:1(M))
5-6:   PKM MG (Med. AP:2/AT:0)

SPECIAL RULES

SPRINT

The brevity code has been transmitted by the OP team and air assets are being vectored in-bound by an orbiting AWACS. From Turn 3, the ODA will have dedicated air support each turn. Use standard TAC/JTAC rules with the OP team counting as both trained and SF. If the OP team is seriously WIA or KIA, other members of the ODA can call in strikes however will not benefit from the trained FAC bonus (although they will still receive the Special Forces bonus).

Each turn when calling in air, roll a 1D6; on a 1-2, an Air Force F-16C with 500 pound JDAMs arrives. On a 3-4, a British Tornado with 1000 pound JDAMs arrives. On a 5, an Air Force A-10 with its internal 30mm cannon and Maverick ATGMs has arrived on-station. On a 6, a B-1B bomber has arrived with a mix of 500 and 1000 pound JDAMs.

An air strike can be called on any Iraqi off-board indirect fire assets and this automatically suppresses the asset for the remainder of the game however the air strike for that turn is considered spent.

THE OP TEAM

The Iraqi forces have a general idea of the location of the OP team but they are considered Hidden in game terms and must be Spotted by Iraqi forces. The OP SR are using a sound suppressed Mk11 sniper rifle and thus can fire without automatically giving away their position. When firing, treat the Mk11 shooter as a sniper. His team mate is maintaining comms and talking in fast air onto targets and thus cannot add his firepower to any attack. The OP receives an In Cover and Solid Cover bonus as they have deployed behind rocks and are using the lay of the land to their advantage.

OUT OF CONTACT MOVEMENT

The Fedayeen may use Out of Contact Movement.

TRENCHES AND THE WADI

The trench-line offers improved cover to Iraqi forces and thus provides a +2 (Solid and improved) to any in cover bonus. The wadi provides a +1 Solid Cover bonus.

HULL DOWN GMVs

The GMVs have been positioned to take best advantage of the natural lay of the land and are considered hull down for purposes of targeting. While they are positioned this way, they can only fire the roof mounted weapon system. If the US player wishes to also fire the forward passenger mounted M240G, the vehicle needs to be moved forward a minimum of 3". If moved, the GMV loses its hull down advantage. The rear M240 can only be fired at targets to the rear 180 degrees of the vehicle. The GMVs are non-up-armored and do not have gunner shields although the gunner does benefit from the standard In Cover (+1) bonus.

ANTI-TANK RPG WARHEADS

Each time an RPG is fired, roll 1D6. If Iraqi regular forces, a roll of 4–6 indicates an AT RPG (Hvy. AP:3/AT:2(M). If Fedayeen or foreign jihadists, a 5–6 indicates an AT RPG.

SCENARIO 18: OBJECTIVE BADGER

The Tier One Special Mission Units of Task Force 20 also conducted their own operations in support of the invasion. These focused on raiding, deception operations and seizing key high value targets and suspect locations. One such operation was the clearance and sensitive site exploitation (SSE) of one of Saddam's lakeside palaces, the Al Qadisiyah Research Centre on the southern shore of the Al Qadisiyah Reservoir. The Al Qadisiyah Research Centre was a suspected WMD site and was added to the target list for the Special Mission Units, Combat Applications Group (Delta) and Naval Special Warfare Development Group, their Ranger security teams and the pilots of 160th Special Operations Aviation Regiment (the Nightstalkers).

On the night of March 26, a task force lifted off consisting of four MH-60Ks carrying the Rangers who would man blocking positions around the target location, two MH-47Es carrying the Task Force 20 operators who would conduct the assault and SSE, two MH-6 Little Birds

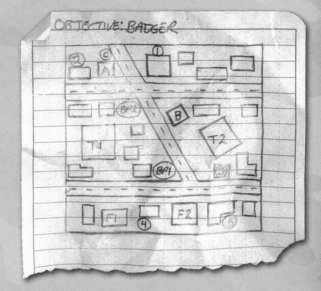

with aerial sniper teams on their bench seats, and two AH-6 and two MH-60L Direct Action Penetrator (DAP) gunships. Two further MH-47s orbited nearby with CSAR and QRF teams on-board. As the first MH-60K touched down, muzzle flashes light up the night as Iraqi gunmen opened fire…

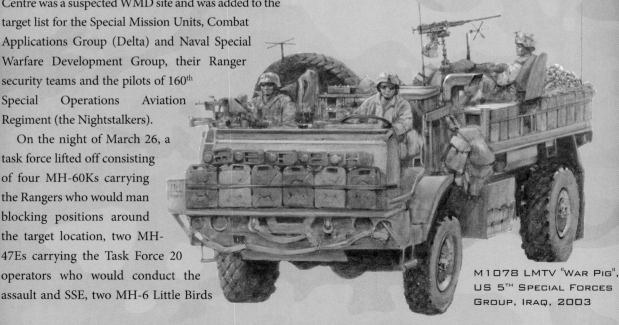

M1078 LMTV "WAR PIG", US 5TH SPECIAL FORCES GROUP, IRAQ, 2003

HISTORICAL OUTCOME

The Rangers successfully maintained their cordon and held off multiple attacks from Iraqi regular and irregular forces with the able assistance of the nimble AH-6s. Further out, the DAP gunships engaged enemy reinforcements, including several technicals, rushing to assist the opposition. The Task Force operators cleared the target buildings despite their MH-47s being engaged by heavy fire on their infiltration. Forty five minutes after landing, the operators were lifted out by the CSAR and QRF helos as their initial lift Chinooks had been too heavily damaged. One Nightstalker and one Ranger were seriously wounded in the operation. Scores of enemy forces were killed however no evidence of WMDs was recovered.

Note that in the real operation, four Ranger blocking positions were established around the target buildings. In this scenario, only two are represented in interests of game play and table size.

SCENARIO INFORMATION

Duration of Game: 8 Turns

Initiative: US for duration of game

Special Conditions:

- Air Defense Environment: Light Air Defense
- Fedayeen are Irregulars

Fog of War: Generated normally by Reaction Tests

Table Size: 4' x 4'

- BP1, BP2: Ranger blocking positions 1 and 2
- F1, F2: Fedayeen positions
- T1, T2: Target Buildings 1 and 2
- 1–5: Hot Spots (Fedayeen RPG Team is located in building by Hot Spot 5)
- A: Iraqi Army Element 1
- B: Iraqi Army Element 2
- C: Iraqi Army PKM GMPG Team

RANGER MISSION

The Rangers must maintain their blocking positions while the Task Force 20 operators clear the target locations. They need to ensure all enemy resistance is suppressed and any reinforcements are engaged or driven back, all the time ensuring civilian and friendly casualties are kept to an absolute minimum. They will have dedicated air support in the form of one MH-6 Little Bird carrying a pair of Delta snipers and one AH-6 Little Bird gunship.

RANGER VICTORY POINTS

- Maintain the cordon at both blocking positions and do not allow any enemy forces within Ranger line of sight to enter the two target buildings: 5pts
- Exfiltrate (complete Turn 8) without any friendly casualties: 5pts
- Exfiltrate (complete Turn 8) without any civilian casualties caused by US fire: 3pts

RANGER FORCE

Ranger Basic Attributes

Initiative Level: D8

Confidence Level: High

Supply Level: Abundant

Body Armor: Standard (1D)

Troop Quality/Morale: D8/D10

Ranger Blocking Position 1

Fire Team One Alpha

1 x Squad Leader w/M4

1 x Fire Team Leader w/M4

1 x Grenadier w/M203 (Lt. AP:1/AT:0)

1 x Gunner w/M249 (Lt. AP:1/AT:0)

1 x Rifleman w/M4 and M136 (AT-4)
(Hvy. AP:4/AT:4(H)

Fire Team Two Alpha

1 x Fire Team Leader w/M4

1 x Grenadier w/M203 (Lt. AP:1/AT:0)

1 x Gunner w/M249 (Lt. AP:1/AT:0)

1 x Rifleman w/M4 and M136 (AT-4)
(Hvy. AP:4/AT:4(H)

Attached Sniper Team

1 x Sniper w/Mk11 (SR-25)

1 x Spotter w/M4

Attached Combat Controller

1 x CCT w/M4

Ranger Blocking Position 2

Fire Team One Bravo

1 x Squad Leader w/M4

1 x Fire Team Leader w/M4

1 x Grenadier w/M203 (Lt. AP:1/AT:0)

1 x Gunner w/M249 (Lt. AP:1/AT:0)

1 x Rifleman w/M4 and M136 (AT-4)
(Hvy. AP:4/AT:4(H)

Fire Team Two Bravo

1 x Fire Team Leader w/M4

1 x Grenadier w/M203 (Lt. AP:1/AT:0)

1 x Gunner w/M249 (Lt. AP:1/AT:0)

1 x Rifleman w/M4 and M136 (AT-4) (Hvy.
AP:4/AT:4(H)

Attached Machine Gun Team

1 x Team Leader w/M4

1 x Gunner w/M240 (Med. AP:2/AT:0)

1 x Assistant Gunner w/M4

Each blocking position deploys with a roll of concertina wire with position shown on the map.

IRAQI MISSION

American helicopters are landing in the vicinity of Saddam's research centre. Iraqi forces have been ordered to protect the site at all costs. The Iraqis have both regular Iraqi Army and Saddam Fedayeen in the area and reinforcements are on the way. Drive back the American Special Forces and shoot down one of their helicopters for the glory of Saddam!

IRAQI VICTORY POINTS

- Each Ranger KIA or captured: 5pts
- Each Ranger Serious WIA: 2pts
- Enter a group of either Iraqi regulars or Fedayeen into one of the two research buildings the Americans are searching: 5pts
- Shoot down an American helicopter: 10pts

IRAQI FORCE

Iraqi Basic Attributes

Initiative Level: D6

Confidence Level: High

Supply Level: Normal

Body Armor: N/A

Troop Quality/Morale: Varies. See below:

Iraqi Regular Army (TQ/Morale D6/D8)

Infantry Element One

5 x riflemen w/AKs

1 x Gunner w/RPK (Lt. AP:1/AT:0)

1 x Gunner w/RPG (Med. AP:2/AT:1(M)

Infantry Element Two

4 x riflemen w/AKs

1 x Gunner w/RPK (Lt. AP:1/AT:0)

1 x Gunner w/RPG (Med. AP:2/AT:1(M)

PKM GPMG Team (no Weapons Team bonus)

1 x Gunner w/PKM (Med. AP:2/AT:0)

1 x Assistant gunner w/AK

Fedayeen (TQ/Morale D6/D12)

Fedayeen Cell One

1 x Fedayeen leader w/AK

1 x Gunner w/RPG (Med. AP:2/AT:1(M)

3 x Irregulars w/AK

Fedayeen Cell Two

1 x Fedayeen leader w/AK

1 x Gunner w/RPG (Med. AP:2/AT:1(M)

4 x Irregulars w/AK

Fedayeen RPG Team One

(no leader nor weapons team bonus)

1 x Gunner w/RPG with AT warheads (Hvy. AP:3/AT:2(M)

1 x Irregular w/AK

Reinforcements

On Turn 2 and every turn thereafter, reinforcements automatically arrive for the Iraqis and arrive on the table as per the Hot Spot rules.

REINFORCEMENT TABLE	
ROLL 1D10: (ALL STATS TQ/MORALE D6/D10)	
1.	4 x Irregulars w/AK, 1 x Leader w/AK
2.	4 x Irregulars w/AK, 1 x Leader w/AK, 1 x Gunner w/Med. Support
3.	1 x Irregular Gunner w/Med. Support, 1 x Irregular w/AK
4.	1 x Irregular SVD Dragunov sniper, 1 x Irregular w/AK
5.	1 x Regular Infantry Element- 5 x AKs, 1 x RPK
6.	1 x Regular Infantry Element- 3 x AKs, 1 x Gunner w/RPK, 1 x Gunner w/Med. Support, 1 x SVD Dragunov
7.	5 x Irregulars w/AK, 1 x Leader w/AK, 1 x Gunner w/Med. Support
8.	6 x Irregulars w/AK, 1 x Leader w/AK, 1 x Gunner w/Med. Support, 1 x RPK gunner
9.	1 x Technical carrying 4 x Irregulars w/AKs, 2 x Irregulars w/Med. Support
10.	1 x Technical mounting DShK (Hvy. AP:4/AT:1(L) with three Irregular crew w/AKs

Medium Support – Roll 1D6 for type:
1: AT RPG (Hvy. AP:3/AT:2(M)
2-4: RPG (Med. AP:2/AT:1(M)
5-6: PKM MG (Med. AP:2/AT:0)

TWO M-6 LITTLE BIRDS LIFT OFF SOMEWHERE OVER IRAQ, 2003

SPECIAL RULES

LITTLE BIRDS

Two Little Birds, one armed AH-6 and one MH-6 carrying two Delta snipers riding on the pods/benches, are flying dedicated air support for the Ranger call signs. The attached CCT must use standard TAC/JTAC rules-if the CCT is seriously WIA or KIA, Ranger squad leaders can call in the Little Birds however will not benefit from the trained FAC bonus.

Each turn when requesting helo support, roll a 1D6; on a 1-4, the MH-6 responds with its snipers. On a 5-6, the AH-6 responds with its two 2.75 inch rocket pods and two miniguns. Snipers mounted in helicopters act exactly as if they are on the ground apart from a die type reduction- in this case the snipers are Delta operators rated at TQ/Morale D12/D12 thus they will shoot from the air as TQ D10.

BUILDINGS

All buildings are rated at 6D8.

CONCERTINA WIRE

Concertina wire takes 1 activation to cross. Units crossing concertina wire may perform no other action while doing so. Units firing at them receive a +1 Troop Quality die shift. Concertina wire may be deployed or recovered in one action by Engineers with proper equipment (gloves, etc.).

OUT OF CONTACT MOVEMENT

The Fedayeen may use Out of Contact Movement.

ANTI-TANK RPG WARHEADS

Each time an RPG is fired, roll 1D6. If Iraqi regular forces, a roll of 4–6 indicates an AT RPG (Hvy. AP:3/AT:2(M)). If Fedayeen or foreign jihadists, a 5–6 indicates an AT RPG.

SCENARIO 19: DEBECKA CROSSROADS

Debecka Crossroads, North of Baghdad, April 6

On 06 Apr 2003, 3 US Army Special Forces Operation Detachments-Alpha (ODA's) engaged and defeated an Iraqi mechanized infantry company supported by tanks at the Debecka Crossroads (north of Baghdad). ODA's 044, 391, and 392 used their Humvees'

HISTORICAL OUTCOME

Lightly armed Special Forces units were able to crush an Iraqi mechanized infantry company with their newly issued Javelin missiles. The battle was further proof of the Coalition's clear technological edge and won the Javelin missile instant and lasting acclaim from the units that fought at the crossroads that day.

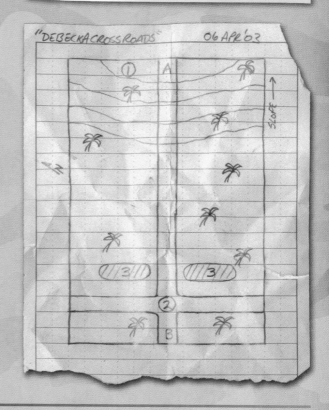

M2 HMG's and Mk19 AGL's, along with Javelin ATGM's and an F18 to defeat the Iraqis. The position they defended would come to be known as "the Alamo."

Scenario Information

Duration of Game: 8 Turns
Initiative: Iraqi force on Turn 1. Test thereafter.
Special Conditions: See Special Rules and Map description above for Hull Down and Alamo positions
- Air Defense Environment: Light Air Defense

Fog of War: Determined normally by Reaction Test rolls
Special Assets:
ODA: Available Air Support (Fast Burners): Due to tasking issues, when fast air is successfully called, it arrives in 1D6 turns, with Turn 1 being the turn it is called.

Table Size: 2' x 3'
- **A:** US exit point.
- **B:** Iraqi reinforcement entry point
- **1:** Alamo Position on a low three to four tier ridge
- **2:** Crossroads
- **3:** Low dirt berms that can provide hull-down positions for tanks

ODA Mission

ODA's 044, 391, and 392 are defending a low ridge known as the "Alamo". They must defend and hold the hill for at least 6 full turns (with no non-pinned, non-suppressed enemy units on it), and must exit the board from point A by the end of Turn 8.

ODA Victory Points
- Each non-pinned ODA team (without vehicle) that exits the Board at A on Turn 7 or 8: 1pt
- Each non-pinned ODA team (with vehicle) that exits the Board at A on Turn 7 or 8: 2pts
- Each Iraqi vehicle destroyed: 3pts

ODA Force
ODA Basic Attributes
Initiative Level: D10
Confidence Level: High
Supply Level: Normal
Body Armor: Standard (1D)
Troop Quality/Morale: D10/D10

The 3 ODA's should be set up initially somewhere on the Alamo ridgeline, facing southwest.

ODA 044
1 x SF NCO (classed as SF JTAC/TAC) w/M4A1/M203 (Lt. AP:1/AT:0)

Team 1
3 x Riflemen w/M4A1
2 x Grenadier w/M4A1/M203 (Lt. AP:1/AT:0)

Team 2
3 x Riflemen w/M4A1
2 x Grenadier w/M4A1/M203 (Lt. AP:1/AT:0)

Transport
1 x Humvee gun-truck mounting M2HB (Hvy. AP:3/AT:1(L)) and passenger side mounted M240G (Med. AP:3/AT:0)
1 x Humvee gun-truck mounting Mk. 19 AGL (Med. AP:3/AT:0) and passenger side mounted M240G (Med. AP:3/AT:0)

ODA 391
Team 1
3 x Riflemen w/M4A1
2 x Grenadier w/M4A1/M203 (Lt. AP:1/AT:0)

Team 2

3 x Riflemen w/M4A1

2 x Grenadier w/M4A1/M203

(Lt. AP:1/AT:0)

Transport

1 x Humvee gun-truck mounting
M2HB (Hvy. AP:3/AT:1(L) and
passenger side mounted M240G (Med. AP:3/AT:0)
1 x Humvee gun-truck mounting Mk. 19 AGL
(Med. AP:3/AT:0) and passenger side mounted
M240G (Med. AP:3/AT:0)

ODA 392:

Team 1

3 x Riflemen w/M4A1

2 x Grenadier w/M4A1/M203 (Lt. AP:1/AT:0)

Team 2

3 x Riflemen w/M4A1

2 x Grenadier w/M4A1/M203 (Lt. AP:1/AT:0)

Transport

1 x Humvee gun-truck mounting M2HB (Hvy.
AP:3/AT:1(L) and passenger side mounted M240G
(Med. AP:3/AT:0)
1 x Humvee gun-truck mounting Mk. 19 AGL
(Med. AP:3/AT:0) and passenger side mounted
M240G (Med. AP:3/AT:0)

IRAQI FORCE MISSION

US infidels have linked up with those Peshmerga dogs.
Attack their weakly defended position, and defeat them
in detail. The fools have no armor support, so this
should be easy!

The Iraqis must seize the hill by the end of Turn 6,
and/or kill as many Americans as possible. To seize

US NAVY F/A-18C HORNET,
BAGHDAD, 2003

the hill, at least one non-pinned, non-
suppressed Iraqi platoon must occupy the
top of the hill, while no non-pinned, non-
suppressed US troops are on it.

IRAQI VICTORY POINTS

- Each US SF team left on the board (with or
  without vehicle): 5pts
- The Alamo is seized by Turn 6: 20pts

IRAQI FORCE

Iraqi Basic Attributes

Initiative Level: D8

Confidence Level: Low

Supply Level: Poor

Body Armor: N/A

Troop Quality/Morale: D8/D8

Mechanized Infantry Platoon 1

This unit starts out within 6" of the southwest
board edge, just to the left of Point B. MTLB's can
lay smoke.

HQ Squad
1 x Platoon Leader w/AK
1 x Platoon Sgt. w/AK
2 x Runners w/AKs

Squad 1
1 x Squad Leader
1 x Gunner w/RPG (Med. AP:2/AT:1(M))
1 x Gunner w/RPK (Lt. AP:1/AT:0)
5 x Riflemen w/AKs

Squad 2
1 x Squad Leader
1 x Gunner w/RPG (Med. AP:2/AT:1(M))
1 x Gunner w/RPK (Lt. AP:1/AT:0)
5 x Riflemen w/AKs

Squad 3
1 x Squad Leader
1 x Gunner w/RPG (Med. AP:2/AT:1(M))
1 x Gunner w/RPK (Lt. AP:1/AT:0)
5 x Riflemen w/AKs

Transport
4 x MTLBs

Mechanized Infantry Platoon 2
This unit starts out within 6" of the southwest board edge, just to the right of Point B. MTLB's can lay smoke.

HQ Squad
1 x Platoon Leader w/AK
1 x Platoon Sgt. w/AK
2 x Runners w/AKs

Squad 1
1 x Squad Leader
1 x Gunner w/RPG (Med. AP:2/AT:1(M))
1 x Gunner w/RPK (Lt. AP:1/AT:0)

5 x Riflemen w/AKs

Squad 2
1 x Squad Leader
1 x Gunner w/RPG (Med. AP:2/AT:1(M))
1 x Gunner w/RPK (Lt. AP:1/AT:0)
5 x Riflemen w/AKs

Squad 3
1 x Squad Leader
1 x Gunner w/RPG (Med. AP:2/AT:1(M))
1 x Gunner w/RPK (Lt. AP:1/AT:0)
5 x Riflemen w/AKs

Transport
4 x MTLBs

Tank Platoon
This unit enters at Point B on Turn 1.
4 x T-55 Tanks

Motorized Infantry Platoon
This unit enters at Point B on Turn 2.

HQ Squad
1 x Platoon Leader w/AK
1 x Platoon Sgt. w/AK
2 x Runners w/AKs

Squad 1
1 x Squad Leader
1 x Gunner w/RPG (Med. AP:2/AT:1(M))
1 x Gunner w/RPK (Lt. AP:1/AT:0)
5 x Riflemen w/AKs

Squad 2
1 x Squad Leader
1 x Gunner w/RPG (Med. AP:2/AT:1(M))

Name	Class	Type	Firepower	MGs	Front Armor	Side Armor	Rear Armor	Deck Armor	Crew
ZSU 57-2	M	T	Twin 57mm AA Auto-Cannons (AP:6/AT:4(M))	3D	3D10	2D10	2D8	1D6	6

1 x Gunner w/RPK (Lt. AP:1/AT:0)

5 x Riflemen w/AKs

Squad 3

1 x Squad Leader

1 x Gunner w/RPG (Med. AP:2/AT:1(M))

1 x Gunner w/RPK (Lt. AP:1/AT:0)

5 x Riflemen w/AKs

Transport

3 x 3 Ton Trucks

Air Defense Unit

This unit enters at Point B on Turn 3.

1 x ZSU 57-2

SPECIAL RULES

JAVELIN ISSUES

Due to issues with the Javelin's Command Launch Units (CLU's) warming-up, each time one is fired, roll a TQ die. If the die is successful, the Javelin may be used as normal, and no further tests are needed for that particular Javelin. If the test is failed, the CLU does not warm up, and the Javelin may not be used

JAVELIN ATGM LAUNCH

that turn. A TQ roll must be attempted the next time the Javelin is used. In addition, each time a Javelin is actually fired, roll a TQ die. If the test is successful, the Javelin may continue to be used. If the test is not successful, that Javelin is out of rounds, and may not be used any further.

FRIENDLY FIRE INCIDENT

When the F18 arrived, its pilot mistook friendly forces to the rear of the Alamo position for the target, and dropped a bomb that caused significant casualties. To account for this, on the turn immediately following the first turn that an F18 arrives, one half-team from ODA 391 must mount their Humvee, and leave the table at Point A (they are called back to help at the scene of the bombing). They will not count toward either side's victory points.

SNIPER!

Most ODA members had some sniper-related training and experience, and the gun trucks each had sniper rifles in them. At the beginning of any turn, any 2 ODA members within 4" of a gun truck may be converted into a sniper team, with the appropriate bonuses and advantages. No more than 1 such team may be so deployed at any given time.

IRAQI SECRET POLICE

Iraqi secret police were known (especially by the Iraqis!) to be operating in the area. Two times during the game, one Iraqi unit may re-roll a failed morale check.

ANTI-TANK RPG WARHEADS

Each time an RPG is fired, roll 1D6. If Iraqi regular forces, a roll of 4–6 indicates an AT RPG (Hvy. AP:3/AT:2(M)). If Fedayeen or foreign jihadists, a 5–6 indicates an AT RPG.

SAMPLE ORGANIZATIONS

Standing military forces devote endless effort and shelves of carefully indexed manuals to record the structure, equipment, and capabilities of their organizations. Looking at a Table of Organization and Equipment (TO&E) for a unit gives one a fine feeling for military precision. Units are clearly defined, soldiers and gear are evenly distributed: Everything and everyone has its place and symmetry is king!

Unfortunately, the world presented by TO&Es exists primarily within those very TO&Es. The concept of "mission based organization" has been gaining steam as an official concept throughout the 20th century and has probably been an unofficial fact of military life since man first started writing down how many spearmen should be in a "proper" formation.

The organizations presented below are rough guidelines for the forces they represent, not inviolable "army lists" handed down from on high. It is not uncommon for commanders to beef up a fireteam with extra men or assets or for a lack of manpower to reduce a squad or fireteam by a third or more in manpower. Commanders may strip the machine-gunners from their squads to use as an ad hoc "weapons squad," or rifle/grenade launchers may be replaced with regular rifles due to restrictive ROEs in an area.

In short, unit organizations are as fluid as the battlefields they fight on. Don't get too caught up in canonical adherence to TO&Es. If you don't have an organization chart for the Third Royal Etruscan Grenadiers, exercise a little common sense – chances are they're organized along the lines of the Cold War Soviet WARPAC forces or similar to modern western forces.

The following organization descriptions represent common units found on the battlefields represented by *Force on Force*.

This force list and the organization descriptions it includes are not exhaustive. They are tailored to reflect the assets and manpower that would be applied to a typical *Force on Force* mission, so they cut off at the Platoon (or equivalent) level.

Organizations are described from the bottom up, starting with the Fireteam and working up to the Platoon.

UNITED KINGDOM

BRITISH ARMY

Initiative Level: D8 to D10
Confidence Level: Confident to High
Supply Level: Normal to Abundant
Body Armor: 1D
Troop Quality/Morale: D8 to D10/D8 to D12

The basic building block of the British Army is the Fireteam. Two Fireteams form a Section. Three Sections form a Platoon.

British Army Section

Fireteam 1

1 x Squad Leader w/SA80

1 x Grenadier w/SA80 UGL (Lt. AP:1/AT:0)

1 x Gunner w/L108A1 (Lt. AP:1/AT:0)

1 x Rifleman w/L86 LSW

Fireteam 2

1 x Asst. Squad Leader w/SA80

1 x Grenadier w/SA80 UGL (Lt. AP:1/AT:0)

1 x Gunner w/L108A1 (Lt. AP:1/AT:0)

1 x Rifleman w/L86 LSW

British Army Rifle Platoon

1 x Platoon Commander w/SA80

1 x Platoon Sgt. w/SA80

3 x British Army Rifle Sections

BRITISH ROYAL MARINES

Initiative Level: D8 to D10

Confidence Level: Confident to High

Supply Level: Normal to Abundant

Body Armor: 1D

Troop Quality/Morale: D8 to D10/D10 to D12

The basic building block of the British Royal Marines is the Fireteam. Two Fireteams form a Section. Three Sections plus a Maneuver Section form a Troop.

British Royal Marine Section

Fireteam 1

1 x Squad Leader w/SA80

1 x Grenadier w/SA80 UGL (Lt. AP:1/AT:0)

1 x Gunner w/L108A1 (Lt. AP:1/AT:0)

1 x Rifleman w/L86

Fireteam 2

1 x Asst. Squad Leader w/SA80

1 x Grenadier w/SA80 UGL (Lt. AP:1/AT:0)

1 x Gunner w/L108A1 (Lt. AP:1/AT:0)

1 x Rifleman w/L86

British Royal Marine Maneuver Support Section

1 x Section Leader w/SA80

1 x Sniper w/L96A1

1 x Gunner w/60mm Mortar (Med.)*

1 x Rifleman w/SA80

*One 60mm mortar per Troop

British Royal Marine Troop

1 x Platoon Commander w/SA80

1 x Platoon Sgt. w/SA80

3 x British Royal Marine Sections

1 x British Royal Marine Maneuver Support Section

UNITED STATES OF AMERICA

UNITED STATES MARINE CORPS (USMC)

Initiative Level: D8 to D10

Confidence Level: Normal to High

Supply Level: Normal

Body Armor: 1D

Troop Quality/Morale: D8 to D10/D10 to D12

The basic building block of the United States Marine Corps is the Fireteam. Three fireteams under a Squad Leader form a Squad. Three Squads under a Platoon Leader form a Platoon.

Typical USMC Rifle Platoon

  USMC Fireteam

    1 x Fireteam Leader w/M16A2

    1 x Grenadier w/M203 (Lt. AP:1/AT:0)

    1 x Gunner w/M249 (Lt. AP:1/AT:0)

    1 x Assistant Gunner w/M16A2

  USMC Squad

    1 x Squad Leader w/M16A2

    3x USMC Fireteams

USMC Platoon

1 x Platoon Leader w/M16A2

1 x Platoon Sgt. w/M16A2

1 x Navy Corpsman w/M16A2

3 x USMC Squads

US ARMY

Initiative Level: D8 to D10

Confidence Level: Normal to High

Supply Level: Abundant

Body Armor: 1D

Troop Quality/Morale: D8 to D10/D8 to D12

The basic building block of the US Army is the Fireteam. Two Fireteams under a Squad Leader make up a Squad. Four Squads make up a Platoon.

US ARMY STRYKER BRIGADE COMBAT TEAM RIFLE PLATOON

US Army Rifle Fireteam

1 x Fireteam Leader w/M4

1 x Grenadier w/M203 (Lt. AP:1/AT:0)

1 x Gunner w/M249 (Lt. AP:1/AT:0)

1 x Assistant Gunner w/M4

US Army Rifle Squad*

1 x Squad Leader w/M4

2 x Rifle Fireteams

Weapons Squad

1 x Squad Leader w/M4

2 x Gunners w/MG240 (Med. AP:3/AT:0)

4 x Assistant Gunners w/M4

*Note that the Squad can split into two MG teams, each of which is treated as a Weapons Team.

US Army Rifle Platoon HQ Squad

1 x Platoon Leader w/M4

1 x Platoon Sgt. w/M4

1 x Radio Operator w/M4

1 x Forward Observer w/M16 or M4

1 x Trauma Expert (Medic) w/M16 or M4 (Medic is attached to platoon, he is not an organic asset)

Transport*

4 x Stryker IFVs

3 x Vehicle Commanders**

4 x Drivers

*It should be noted that the four Strykers have a carrying capacity of 44 personnel, but the organization above lists 45 organic personnel and an attached medic for a total of 46 personnel. It is unusual for all personnel to be used in a given operation as some are tactical cross-loaded to other units in the company, are not necessary to the operation, or are otherwise unavailable.

**The vacant Vehicle Commander position can be filled by one of the platoon's leaders.

US Army Rifle Platoon

1 x Rifle Platoon HQ Squad

3 x Rifle Squads

1 x Weapon Squad

US ARMY MECHANIZED RIFLE PLATOON – BRADLEY FIGHTING VEHICLES (BFVs)

US Army Rifle Fireteam

1 x Fireteam Leader w/M4

1 x Grenadier w/M203 (Lt. AP:1/AT:0)

1 x Gunner w/M249 (Lt. AP:1/AT:0)

1 x Assistant Gunner w/M4

US Army Rifle Squad*

1 x Squad Leader w/M4

2 x Rifle Fireteams

Weapons Squad

1 x Squad Leader w/M4

2 x Gunners w/MG240 (Med. AP:3/AT:0)

4 x Assistant Gunners w/M4

*Note that the Squad can split into two MG teams, each of which is treated as a Weapons Team.

US Army Rifle Platoon HQ Squad

1 x Platoon Leader w/M4

1 x Platoon Sgt. w/M4

1 x Radio Operator w/M4

1 x Forward Observer w/M16 or M4

1 x Trauma Expert (Medic) w/M16 or M4 (Medic is attached to platoon, he is not an organic asset)

Transport

4 x BFVs w/M4

4 x Vehicle Commanders w/M4

4 x Drivers w/M4

4 x Gunners w/M4

1 x Alternate Gunner w/M4

US Army Rifle Platoon

1 x Rifle Platoon HQ Squad

3 x Rifle Squads

1 x Weapon Squad

THE IRAQI MILITARY AND PARAMILITARY

The Iraqi Army, and particularly the Republican Guard, was ravaged during the "First Gulf War." In the following years, both forces were further degraded by the growing paranoia of their commander in chief, Saddam Hussein.

Hussein feared a military coup might oust him from power and he resorted to extra-ordinarily self-destructive measures to guard against such an eventuality: Communications between organizations was purposefully compromised, regular army units were forced to compete against more favored paramilitary organizations (Al-Qudds, the Ba'ath militias, and the Saddam Fedayeen) while draconian edicts made it far safer to conceal any problems regarding manning, supply or quality of gear than to admit any shortcomings. Add to this the endemic corruption that characterized most of the Iraqi officer corps and the recipe for chaos is complete.

As a result of these factors and others, Coalition forces often found defensive positions poorly manned or incompetently sited. While many Iraqi units did put up a stiff fight, they did so handicapped by a lack of training, military discipline, and effective battlefield command. To compound their problems, paramilitary units such as the Saddam Fedayeen were routinely assigned to "stiffen" the army that Hussein's paranoia had reduced to a shadow of its former self. Officers and troops were bullied by the Fedayeen fanatics to ignore what training they had and attack in disorganized masses that were quickly cut down by the Coalition's disciplined and well directed fire.

Realistically, no credible "order of battle" exists for Iraqi forces involved in most engagements. They were a mixture of regular army, reservists, volunteers, and fanatical paramilitary organizations.

We suggest that, for simplicity's sake, Iraqi forces be represented by small teams of four or five soldiers/fighters. No higher level of organization is needed, as most Iraqi units were not under particularly effective command and control – each band of soldiers simply did the best they could in the circumstances in which they found themselves.

IRAQI REGULAR ARMY

Initiative Level: D6 to D8
Confidence Level: Low to Normal
Supply Level: Low to Normal
Body Armor: N/A
Troop Quality/Morale: D6 to D8/D6 to D8

IRAQI REPUBLICAN GUARD

Initiative Level: D8
Confidence Level: Low to Normal
Supply Level: Low to Normal
Body Armor: N/A
Troop Quality/Morale: D8/D8

IRAQI PARAMILITARY ORGANIZATIONS

Initiative Level: D6
Confidence Level: High
Supply Level: Low to Normal
Body Armor: N/A
Troop Quality/Morale: D6/D10 to D12

BIBLIOGRAPHY

Sgt. 1st Class Antenori, Halbersstadt. *Roughneck Nine-One: The Extraordinary Story of a Special Forces A-Team at War.* New York: St. Martin's Press, 2006.

Atkinson, Rick. *In the Company of Soldiers: A Chronicle of Combat.* New York: Henry Holt & Company, 2004.

Col. Fontenot, Lt. Col. Degen, Lt. Col. Tohn. *On Point.* Annapolis: Naval Institute Press, 2005.

Fick, Nathaniel. *One Bullet Away: The Making of a Marine Officer.* New York: Houghton-Mifflin, 2005.

Gordon, Gen. Trainor. *Cobra II: The Inside Story of the Invasion and Occupation of Iraq.* New York: Pantheon Books, 2006.

John Keegan. *The Iraq War*, Vintage Books, 2005

Lacey, Jim. *Take Down: The 3rd Infantry Division's Twenty One Day Assault on Baghdad.* Annapolis: Naval Institute Press, 2007.

Lowry, Richard S. *Marines in the Garden of Eden: The True Story of Seven Bloody Days in Iraq.* New York: Berkley Caliber, 2006.

Muray, Scales. *The Iraq War: A Military History.* Cambridge & London: The Belknap Press of Harvard University Press, 2003.

Neville, Leigh. *Special Operations Forces in Iraq.* Oxford: Osprey Publishing, 2008

Pritchard, Tim. *Ambush Alley: The Most Extraordinary Battle of the Iraq War.* New York: Ballantine Books, 2005.

Robinson, Linda. *Masters of Chaos: The Secret History of the Special Forces.* New York: Public Affairs, 2004.

West, Bing. *The March Up: Taking Baghdad with the United States Marines.* New York: Bantam Dell, 2003.

Wright, Evan. *Generation Kill: Devil Dogs, Iceman, Captain America and the New Face of American War.* New York: G.P. Putnam and Sons, 2004.

Zucchino, David. *Thunder Run: The Armored Strike to Capture Baghdad.* New York: Grove Press, 2004.

ARTWORK REFERENCES

Pg.5 *HH-60L Medevac Helicopter, Iraq, 2003*, by Ian Palmer © Osprey Publishing Ltd. Taken from New Vanguard 116: *Sikorsky UH-60 Black Hawk*.

Pg.9 *Challenger 2 MBT, Basra, 2003*, by Tony Bryan © Osprey Publishing Ltd. Taken from New Vanguard 112: *Challenger 2 Main Battle Tank 1987–2006*.

Pg.14 *Challenger Armoured Repair and Recovery Vehicle, Al Faw Peninsula, 2003*, by Tony Bryan © Osprey Publishing Ltd. Taken from New Vanguard 112: *Challenger 2 Main Battle Tank 1987–2006*.

Pg.19 *USMC AH-1W Super Cobra in Iraq, 2003*, by Jim Laurier © Osprey Publishing Ltd. Taken from New Vanguard 125: *Huey Cobra Gunships*.

Pg.23 *US Marine, Iraq, 2003*, by Howard Gerrard © Osprey Publishing Ltd. Taken from Warrior 106: *US Marine in Iraq: Operation Iraqi Freedom, 2003*.

Pg.27 *USMC, An Nasiriyah, 2003*, by Howard Gerrard © Osprey Publishing Ltd. Taken from Warrior 106: *US Marine in Iraq: Operation Iraqi Freedom, 2003*.

Pg.38 *US Infantryman, Baghdad, 2004*, by Howard Gerrard © Osprey Publishing Ltd. Taken from Warrior 113: *US Army Soldier*.

Pg.41 *US Fireteam, Baghdad, 2004*, by Howard Gerrard © Osprey Publishing Ltd. Taken from Warrior 113: *US Army Soldier*.

Pg.45 *US Infantry raid a bombmaking facility, Baghdad, 2003*, by Howard Gerrard © Osprey Publishing Ltd. Taken from Warrior 113: *US Army Soldier*.

Pg.49 *Combat at Karbala, 2004*, by Howard Gerrard © Osprey Publishing Ltd. Taken from Warrior 113: *US Army Soldier*.

Pg. 52 *US Navy SEALs, Persian Gulf, 2003*, by Michael Welply © Osprey Publishing Ltd. Taken from Elite 113: *US Navy SEALs*.

Pg.55 *US Navy SEAL, Operation* Iraqi Freedom, *2003*, by Michael Welply © Osprey Publishing Ltd. Taken from Elite 113: *US Navy SEALs*.

Pg.60 *US Navy SEAL, Operation* Iraqi Freedom, *2003*, by Michael Welply © Osprey Publishing Ltd. Taken from Elite 113: *US Navy SEALs*.

Pg.65 *US Navy SEAL, Operation* Iraqi Freedom, *2003*, by Michael Welply © Osprey Publishing Ltd. Taken from Elite 113: *US Navy SEALs*.

Pg.68 *US Special Forces, Iraq, 2003*, by Richard Hook © Osprey Publishing Ltd. Taken from Elite 170: *Special Operations Forces in Iraq*.

Pg.75 *British Special Forces Support Group Operator, Iraq, 2003*, by Richard Hook © Osprey Publishing Ltd. Taken from Elite 170: *Special Operations Forces in Iraq*.

Pg.79 *US Navy SEAL Team 4 Operator, Iraq, 2003*, by Richard Hook © Osprey Publishing Ltd. Taken from Elite 170: *Special Operations Forces in Iraq*.

Pg.90 *M1078 LMTV "War Pig", US 5th Special Forces Group, Iraq, 2003*, by Richard Hook © Osprey Publishing Ltd. Taken from Elite 170: *Special Operations Forces in Iraq*.

Pg.96 *US Navy F/A-18C Hornet, Baghdad, 2003*, by Mark Postlethwaite © Osprey Publishing Ltd. Taken from Combat Aircraft 46: *US Navy Hornet Units of Operation* Iraqi Freedom *(Part One)*.